Michael Humphries
February 11th 1975

AF593324

CUMBRIAN VILLAGES

THE VILLAGE SERIES

Cotswold Villages
June Lewis

Cumbrian Villages
Kenneth Smith

Devon Villages
S. H. Burton

Lancashire Villages
Jessica Lofthouse

Suffolk Villages
Allan Jobson

Surrey Villages
Derek Pitt and Michael Shaw

Yorkshire Villages
G. Bernard Wood

Cumbrian Villages

KENNETH SMITH

ROBERT HALE · LONDON

© *Kenneth Smith 1973*
First published in Great Britain 1973

ISBN 0 7091 4175 0

Robert Hale & Company
63 Old Brompton Road
London S.W.7

PRINTED IN GREAT BRITAIN BY
CLARKE, DOBLE & BRENDON LTD.
PLYMOUTH

Contents

Illustrations

TO MY WIFE MARGARET

Introduction

THIS is neither a guide-book nor a gazetteer. Inevitably it has some of the characteristics of both, but it will not tell you precisely where a place is situated, nor how best to get to it. My aim has been to set out the principal features of interest in the various villages of the area. Too many motorists, and it is mainly for motorists this book has been written, stick to main roads exclusively, or point their bonnets towards some known seaside resort or beauty spot and try to get there as quickly as possible. Villages they notice only if they see ice cream on sale, or find themselves short of petrol. Yet it was from the villages that much of our history came. They were the basic human settlements and, in fact, it was their inhabitants who in the end made our towns and cities what they are, by flocking to them for work and other amenities as the country's emphasis changed from agricultural and rural to industrial and urban. Now the city folk are trekking back again to buy up the village cottages for week-end retreats where they can find quietness and a lessening of the pressures of modern life.

The area covered by the word 'Cumbrian' in the title is the area embraced by the new administrative county of Cumbria. By chance or design it is also almost identical with the boundaries of the Diocese of Carlisle. It takes in the whole of Cumberland and Westmorland, and also that part of north Lancashire commonly referred to as 'north of the Sands'—that is to the north of Morecambe Bay. It includes, therefore, the whole of the Lake District. Many of the villages in the northern part of the region did not appear in Domesday Book, for the simple reason that at the time of William the Conqueror, Carlisle and a large area around

Cumbrian Villages

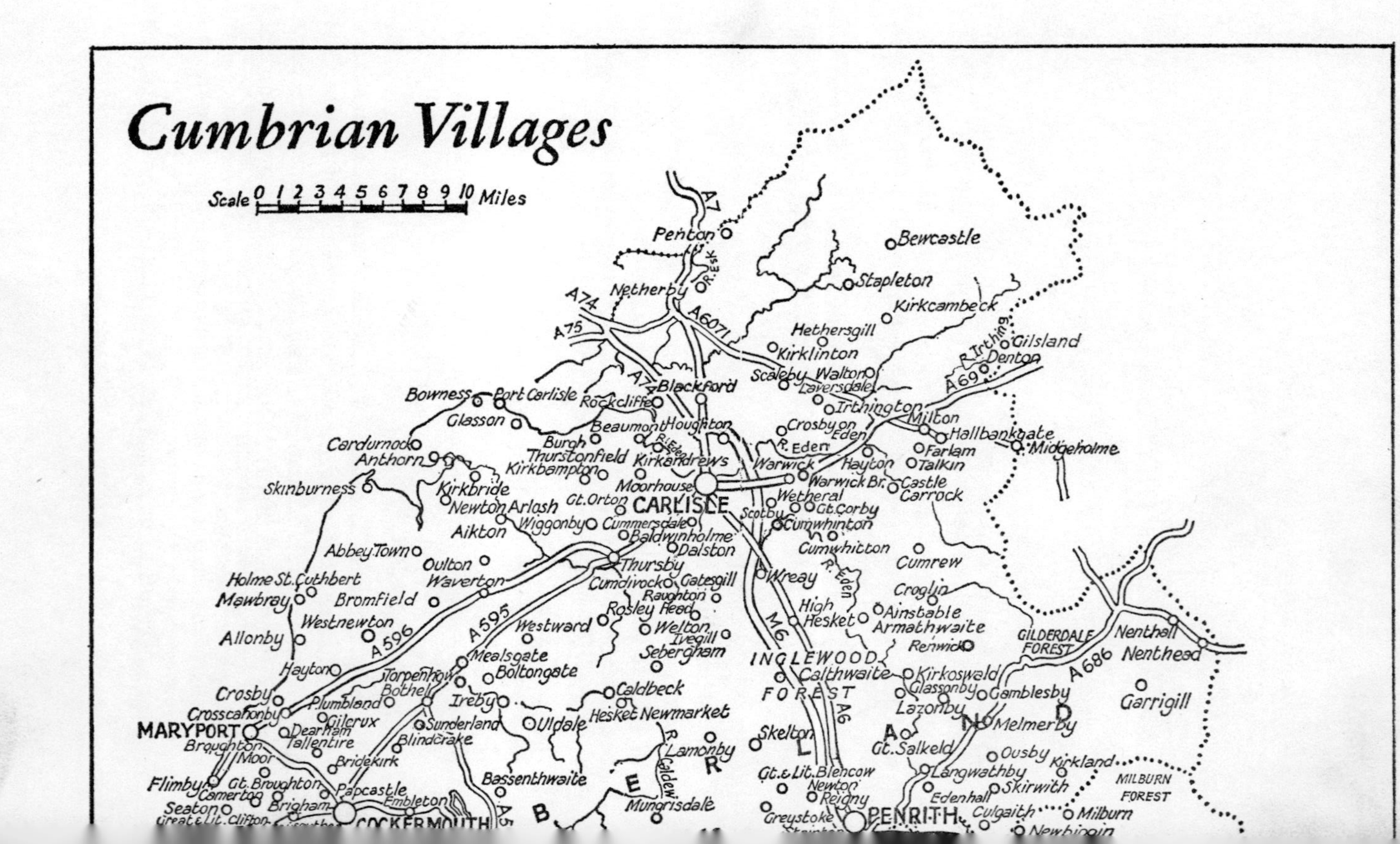

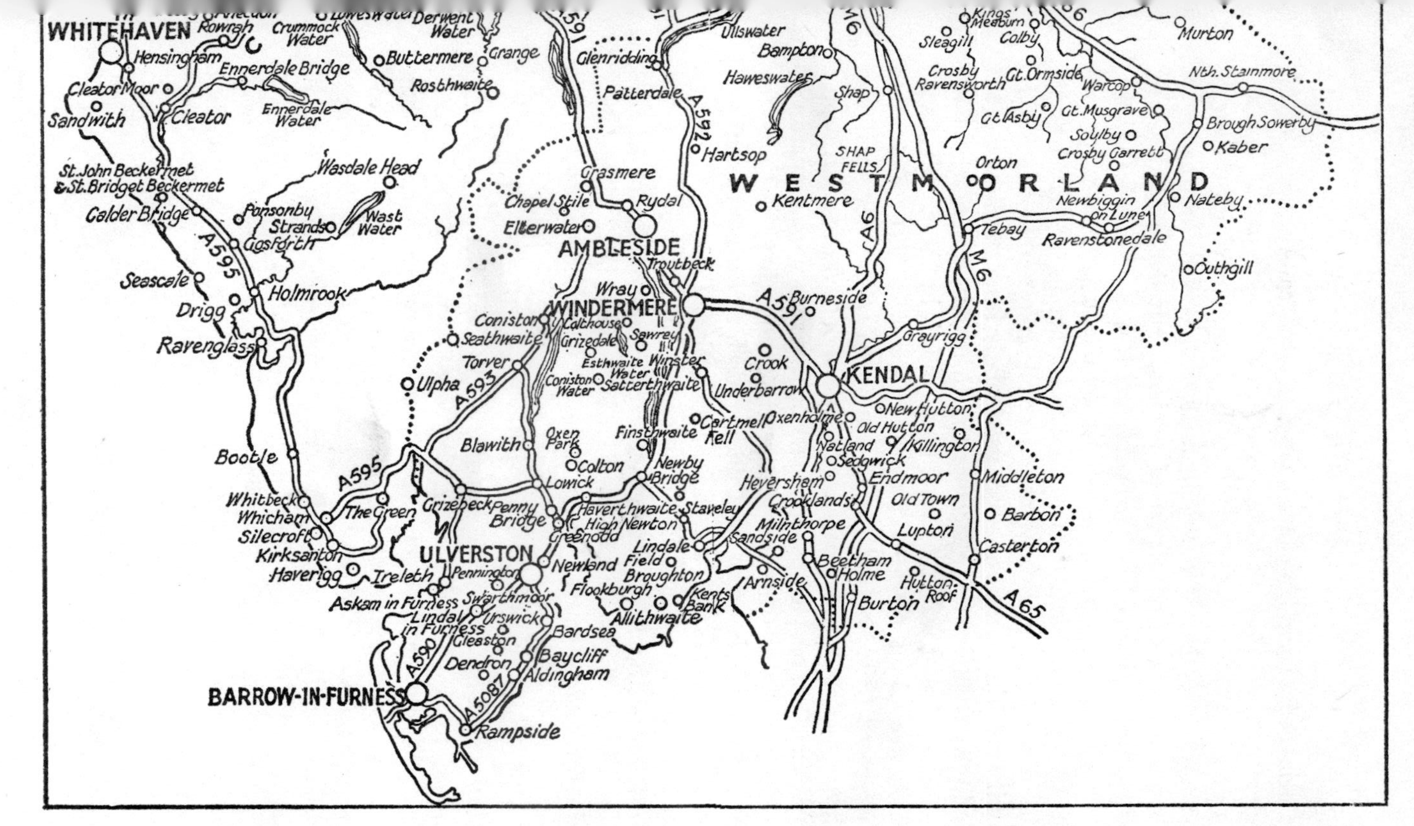

WHITEHAVEN
Hensingham
Rowrah
Cleator Moor
Sandwith
Cleator
Ennerdale Bridge
Ennerdale Water
Crummock Water
Derwent Water
Buttermere
Grange
Rosthwaite
St. John Beckermet & St. Bridget Beckermet
Calder Bridge
Wasdale Head
Wast Water
Ponsonby
Strands
Gosforth
A595
Seascale
Holmrook
Drigg
Ravenglass
Bootle
Whitbeck
Whicham
Silecroft
Kirksanton
Haverigg
The Green
Grizebeck
Treleth
Askam in Furness
Lindal in Furness
BARROW-IN-FURNESS
Rampside
A590
A5087
Dendron
Gleaston
Urswick
Swarthmoor
Pennington
ULVERSTON
Newland
Bardsea
Baycliff
Aldingham
Penny Bridge
Greenodd
Blawith
Lowick
Colton
Oxen Park
Ulpha
Torver
A593
Seathwaite
Coniston
Coniston Water
Glenridding
Patterdale
A592
Hartsop
Grasmere
Chapel Stile
Rydal
Elterwater
AMBLESIDE
Troutbeck
Wray
WINDERMERE
Colthouse
Grizedale
Sawrey
Esthwaite Water
Winster
Satterthwaite
Finsthwaite
Newby Bridge
Haverthwaite
High Newton
Staveley
Lindale
Field Broughton
Flookburgh
Allithwaite
Kents Bank
Cartmel Fell
Underbarrow
Crook
A591
Burneside
KENDAL
Oxenholme
Grayrigg
Ullswater
Bampton
Haweswater
Shap
SHAP FELLS
A6
M6
WESTMORLAND
Kentmere
Orton
Tebay
Ravenstonedale
Newbiggin on Lune
Outhgill
Nateby
Kaber
Brough Sowerby
Nth. Stainmore
Murton
Warcop
Gt. Musgrave
Soulby
Crosby Garrett
Gt. Asby
Gt. Ormside
Crosby Ravensworth
Sleagill
Kings Meaburn
Colby
New Hutton
Old Hutton
Killington
Natland
Sedgwick
Endmoor
Heversham
Crooklands
Milnthorpe
Sandside
Arnside
Beetham
Holme
Burton
Old Town
Lupton
Hutton Roof
Middleton
Barbon
Casterton
A65

it belonged to the king of Scotland. Shakespeare in his *Macbeth* refers to the Prince of Cumberland as successor to the Scottish throne just as we, today, refer to the Prince of Wales as heir to our own sovereign. It was William II who decided that the region should be considered a part of England. His decision was hotly and actively disputed by the Scots, and it was not until the mid-thirteenth century that the whole of Cumbria became permanently English. From then on, for a further five hundred years, the people of Cumbria were subjected to repeated and savage raids from the Scots, and more particularly from the Border clans and reivers who owned allegiance to neither Scotland nor England.

Bounded as it was, therefore, to the north by the hostile Scots; to the west by the sea; and to the east and south by mountains (separated from England as has often been said by forty miles of sheep and Shap), the greater part of the region was to a fair degree isolated. The people looked on themselves as a race apart and mistrusted strangers. It is perhaps significant that the Cumbrian dialect has one hundred and nine words for beating, or bashing; sixty-seven words for a fool or weak-minded person; but very few for affection! Cumbria was, of course, the last area of England to suffer warfare, for through the region passed Prince Charles Edward Stuart (Bonnie Prince Charlie) at the head of his army of Highlanders in the 1745 Jacobite Rebellion. They entered England on 8th November and advanced southwards, taking Carlisle on the 17th and proclaiming James III King of England. They continued through Penrith, Shap and Kendal and into Lancashire. By 15th December they were back in Kendal in hasty retreat from the Duke of Cumberland's army and the Rebellion was over. It seems appropriate somehow that Prince Charlie's illegitimate daughter should be buried here in the quiet churchyard at Finsthwaite. The Rebellion had, however, made people in the rest of England aware as they never had been before of the north-western counties. At the time Londoners knew far more about France, Italy, Germany and even the Indies and America than they did about the Lake District. As roads improved and communications developed the visitors started to come, although it was not until 1763 that the first stage coach could travel over Shap. Then with the disturbances in France which culminated in the French Revolution preventing the Grand Tour of the continent the trickle of visitors grew steadily. Now the M6 motorway, opened in its entirety from south to north of the region in 1970, has thrown Cumbria wide open to visitors.

One of the biggest difficulties in writing this book was in deciding what was a village and should be included. My own rough definition of a village would be a place with a church, a pub, a village store (but probably no opportunity to exercise choice in shopping), and some form of communal life. On the whole anything bigger than this (Longtown, Brampton, Silloth, Wigton, Millom, Penrith, Appleby, Ambleside, Ulverston, Cartmel, etc. etc.) is not included; anything smaller is looked on as a hamlet and similarly excluded. The border line, however, is very indeterminate, and in doubtful cases I have more or less accepted the definition given by Bartholomew's Gazetteer. Three hundred and twenty-seven places seemed to merit inclusion and this gave an approximate average of two hundred words per village. This limiting factor is mentioned in order to counter any charges of superficiality which may be levelled at me. I have mentioned the things that struck me as interesting or significant; any known legends or important historical data connected with a place; natives who achieved fame in some sphere; and so on. If this nucleus sparks off anyone else to make a study in greater depth, as for example has been carried out by some Women's Institutes, I shall feel that my own effort has been worthwhile. Lack of space has prevented me from including the histories of the various families which have identified themselves with so many of our villages, or of describing castles and other buildings which may be passed along the way but are not part of the village concerned. In the course of writing this book I have visited every one of the villages mentioned in it.

Perhaps it may seem that too much stress has been laid on the village churches. I do not see how it could have been otherwise. The church, before and after the Reformation, has almost invariably been the focal point of the village's history and activity. In the church the village's famous people were commemorated or buried; its traditions and continuity were preserved. It has fascinated me, for example, to unfold the story of St. Kentigern as I have travelled around. This Scottish saint was obviously very much loved in Cumbria. In no other part of England so far as I can ascertain are there any churches dedicated to him. In this region there are at least ten—eight within the scope of this book (Kirkcambeck, Irthington, Grinsdale, Bromfield, Caldbeck, Dearham, Crosthwaite and Mungrisdale—all be it noted in Cumberland). Most of the known facts and stories of his life are depicted in stained glass windows in one church or another. As a child he was adopted by the hermit St. Servan. The other children became jealous of Kentigern's (or Mungo as his master affectionately called him) special relationship with the saint. In spite they killed a robin, of which their master was fond, intending to put the blame on Kentigern. The boy is said to have breathed on the bird and brought it back to life. He is shown with the bird in his hand in the east window at Burneside, and a modern window at Winster shows the robin perched on his forefinger. He travelled through Strathclyde, of which Cumberland was then a part, preaching to the people. A fine window in St. Giles church, Great Orton, shows him 'Christianizing Cumbria A.D. 590', as does a window at Irthington church. He became the patron saint of Glasgow and is depicted with his cathedral in a window at Burgh-by-Sands. One of the most famous stories concerning him is of the ring given by the Scottish King Roderick to his wife. She gave it to a knight, on whose finger the King saw it and, taking it off while the knight slept, threw it into the Clyde. He then asked his wife for the return of the ring on penalty of death, convinced of her infidelity. She sought Kentigern's help and the saint had a salmon caught and cut open, and there was the ring which he returned to the queen. This legend is hinted at by the fish carved above the door at Kirkcambeck church and in windows at Bowness-on-Solway and at Abbeytown. In extreme old age the saint's jaw muscles became so weak that his jaw could be kept closed only by a bandage. This, according to good authority, is depicted in a medallion in the west window at Bromfield. There are, of course, other depictions of the saint in several churches. It would be an interesting project to do a study of church dedications, or the ones to a specific saint. If there are, for example, only ten dedications to St. Patrick in English churches, as I have been told, three of these come into this book—Bampton, Patterdale and Preston Patrick (Crooklands). There are, of course, very many St. Cuthberts, St. Marys, and All Saints. There is a St. Theobald, a St. Giles, and a St. Hilda. There is even a church dedicated (for want of a better word) to a scientist—the John Dalton Memorial church near Eaglesfield. There is a church (Greystoke) which has a depiction of a red devil in one of its windows. There is said to be only one other example of this in England. There is a church (Whicham) with a Victoria Cross on display.

It is regretted that it has not been possible to introduce much about the Cumbrian character. Perhaps it may be summed up in the words I heard an old farmer say in a village pub when the talk had turned to religion. Asked what his religion was he paused and commented—"theer's mony different roads to t' cattle mart, but when tha gets theer they don't ask which road tha's come by, but how good's thi stock?" While on this theme, it will be obvious throughout this book what a great hold Wesleyanism had on the dalesfolk. The chapels in the various villages illustrate the confusion which existed in the history of Methodism. It was founded by John Wesley, but in 1797 the Methodist New Connexion separated from Wesleyan Methodism. There were other secessions from Wesleyan Methodism from time to time, including the revival movement in 1811 of Primitive Methodism. In 1857 many of the seceders came together to form the United Methodist Free churches, which joined with others, for example the New Connexion, in 1907 to become the United Methodist church. Then in 1932 this body united with the original Wesleyan Methodists and the Primitive Methodists to form the Methodist Church of Great Britain. This last merger resulted in the closure of many chapels. Some have been converted into private houses, some stand deserted. The southern part of the region, Furness and around Ulverston in particular, played a tremendous part in the origin of the Society of Friends (Quakers).

Finally a word on the arrangement of the book. The M6 motorway splits the region into two parts and, therefore, the book has been so divided. The first four chapters cover those villages east of the motorway—between it and the Pennine range, and along the beautiful Eden valley. The remaining eight chapters are about the area west of the motorway, describing the villages along the Solway Firth, down the long coastal strip, the Lake District, and around the north end of Morecambe Bay. Little, if any, clue is given as to how to get to any village. Most can be reached within two hours from anywhere in the region. Some intelligent map-reading will produce many varied ways of getting from one village to another, and will introduce the motorist to some of the most delightful and quiet lanes along which it has ever been his pleasure to drive.

Apart from personal knowledge and observation, my chief sources of information have been the standard histories of the three counties, Bulmer's directories, Pevsner's "Buildings of England" series, Mee's "The King's England" series, and the periodical *Cumbria.* I have attempted to verify facts and dates. Local legends have been included for their own intrinsic interest. All opinions expressed are my own only, unless otherwise attributed.

K.S.

Carlisle

I

The Wild North-east

THIS chapter concerns itself with the villages of the wild north-east—the area east of the M6 motorway and the A74, north of the A69 Carlisle–Newcastle road, and extending to the Scottish and Northumberland borders. Much of it is land which for some six hundred years knew little peace. For much of that time it was known as the Debatable Land, the English/Scottish border being far from precise, and was occupied by border clans accepting allegiance to neither country, and raiding and plundering indiscriminately at one time to the south, at another to the north. The Armstrongs, the Grahams, and the Eliots were the most known and feared names, and these surnames are still among the most common in this part of the county. A history such as this, with few men's hands offered in friendship, bred an independent and suspicious attitude which has by no means disappeared to this day. (I remember well walking down a quiet lane near Longtown when a sturdy and unsmiling boy of about four toddled out of a farm gate. "What's yoor name?" he demanded instantly and belligerently.) It also produced villages which have less communal cohesion than one usually expects in a place called a village. Safety seemed to lie in separation, in trusting no man, in standing alone.

Such a 'village' is Shopford, or Bewcastle. On some maps Bewcastle is not shown as a place, yet some local signposts point to 'Bewcastle', others to 'Shopford'. It is approached through some of the loveliest unspoilt countryside in the county, past Askerton Castle, now a farmhouse. On one of the barns at Askerton there is an unusual weather vane; a man holding a dog on a leash.

Bewcastle church stands lonely to the north. The gazetteer lists the village as Shopford, named from a shop, probably a blacksmith's shop, at the crossing, but it is little more than a scattering of a very few farms and houses. The pub is the 'Lime Kiln' and the post office, more like a hen house, stands almost opposite at the entrance to Bush Farm. North of the church are the ruins of the old castle, Bueth's Castle, built with stones from the former Roman settlement from which Bewcastle gets its name. The castle was destroyed by Cromwell. The ancient church, dedicated to St. Cuthbert, has no windows at all on the north side. Perhaps this was to keep out the biting northern weather. The glory of the place is the famous Bewcastle Cross, still standing upright on the south side of the church. The first thing one marvels at is the amazingly good state of preservation of the carvings, exposed as they have been to 1,300 years of wild weather across the fells. These same fells struck terror to the heart of Daniel Defoe, the author of *Robinson Crusoe*, when he adventured there in 1762. The western face of the Cross carries what at least one authority considers to be the earliest carving in England of Christ. The top part of the Cross is missing. It was sent to Camden, the Elizabethan historian, and subsequently lost. There is a theory that St. Patrick was born at Bewcastle of a native woman by a Roman officer. At Christianbury Crag, approximately five miles to the north and just inside the county boundary, roams one of the very few herds of wild goats in the country.

On a bleak day one can well understand why this was part of the Debatable Land, wanted by neither England nor Scotland. In fact the reputation of Bewcastle folk was so low at one time that there existed a byelaw in Newcastle prohibiting the freemen of that city from apprenticing any youth from Bewcastle. However, the Mayor of Newcastle in 1900–1, John Beattie (1844–1920), was born at Bewcastle. Today good, though narrow, roads make a truly delightful route over the present Scottish border to Newcastleton.

Another lonely church serving a scattered community of houses and farms over a radius of about two miles is Stapleton, not far south-west of Bewcastle. The church, dedicated to St. Mary, was built in 1830 on the site of an older one. There has, in fact, been one here since the thirteenth century. It is unexpectedly large, light and airy, with an attractive flat ceiling. The roll of honour in the church gives the names of survivors, as well as of those who were killed in the 1914–18 war. This is a not uncommon practice in this part of the area. On the south side of the church and close to it is the grave of Robert Forrester, dated 1598. The school is nearby but the parish hall (1909) is a little distance away on the Hethersgill road.

About the same distance from Bewcastle, but in a more southerly direction, is the village of Kirkcambeck—'the church on the crooked stream'. The village straggles up a hill, with the pub, the 'Wheatsheaf Inn', at the bottom and the church and a few more houses at the top. It has the air of a lonely, forgotten place. A stone arch on a mound close by the church is part of an older church. The present one, built in 1885, is one of those dedicated to St. Kentigern and has above its porch a carving of the salmon in the story which I have told in the introduction to this book.

Hethersgill, making an isosceles triangle with Kirkcambeck and Stapleton, is a village spreadeagled on a crossroads. One road has the pub, 'The Black Lion'; another the Wesleyan church (1901); the third has a recent village hall, quite large and prosperous looking; while the fourth road has the school-room type church, dedicated to St. Mary and built in 1876. The war memorial is in the churchyard. The village school is a fair way to the west of the village. About a mile down the road south of St. Mary's church is the farm of Fordlands. There was born George Graham (*c.* 1673–1751), one of the very few Cumbrians to be buried in Westminster Abbey. He is recorded as leaving Cumberland at the age of fifteen and, according to some authorities, walking to London. He became apprenticed to a clock-maker and later worked with the famous Thomas Tompion, marrying his niece and subsequently, in 1713, taking over his business. He contributed more to horology and astronomy than the better known Tompion, and his dead-beat escapement and mercury pendulum were unchallenged for accuracy for nearly 200 years. He is buried in the same grave in Westminster Abbey as Tompion.

Westward again is Kirklinton, 'the place by the Lyne with a church', another parish rather than a village in the true sense. The church, of St. Cuthbert, is beautifully set amidst wooded fields. Approaching it, particularly from the south-west, it seems to stand in a commanding position but its tower looks oddly top-heavy. It was built in 1845 on the site of an older church whose ancient arch is preserved in the west end of the present church. There is no surrounding village, and Kirklinton Hall lies pathetically empty and derelict. At Sikeside to the south-east are the remains of a Friends Meeting House built in 1736. The pews and pulpit were still inside twenty-five years ago, but it is now used as a store for agricultural machinery.

Scaleby, south of Kirklinton, is listed as a village; but it is difficult to tell which cluster of houses is precisely Scaleby. Scaleby Post Office is at Barclose, where is also the pub with an unusual inn-sign and the equally unusual name of 'The Heilk Moon' (almost certainly the whole, or full, moon, from the Icelandic 'heill'). The Bewcastle Fox Hounds sometimes meet at this pub. In a garden beside the road nearby is a fine monkey-puzzle tree. Scaleby church, of All Saints, is a short distance away with another group of houses. The rather bleak little church dates from the thirteenth century and was restored in 1861. Its font is dated 1707, the year of the Act of Union between England and Scotland. Close to it is the village hall (1895) and war memorial, another which lists the names of survivors as well as those who fell. At Scaleby Hill to the west early converts to Wesleyan Methodism, in 1773, were persecuted. They met in each others' homes until they were able to build a tiny chapel in 1828. It is still in use and beautifully kept. Scaleby Castle, due south of the village, was besieged during the Civil War. It is now the home of Lord Henley.

Laversdale not far away, although called a village is little more than a sprinkling of farms and houses, mainly new. There is a pub, the 'Dog and Gun', and a general store, but no church nor any sign of communal life, although the old school was turned into a village hall and I am told activities do take place there. Laver Beck rises here.

On the other side of the line of Hadrian's Wall from Laversdale is the delightful village of Irthington set astride a quiet, winding road, which drops down into the village whichever way one approaches. It is, simply, 'the place on the river Irthing' and, as might be expected, many of the stones in the Norman church of

St. Kentigern are taken from the Wall and the nearby Roman station. It is a shame to have to refute the claim, made in one of the stained glass windows, that a certain Robert Bowman died in 1823 at the wonderful age of 118! Sadly, this is not true. Another Victorian window carries two medallions depicting St. Kentigern—one is a full length figure, the other shows him preaching to the Britons. The separate clock tower was added to the church in 1896–7.

Carlisle Airport lies between Irthington and Crosby-on-Eden. During Bonnie Prince Charlie's advance into England in 1745 General Wade found it impossible to move his troops quickly across from Newcastle to Carlisle to engage the Prince. Consequently, in 1751 to 1758, he built what is still often called 'the military road', largely following the route of Hadrian's Wall. On this road, and only a few miles east of the new motorway, stands Crosby. It is a village of old and new houses on both sides of a winding portion of the road, set amidst the farms and silos on flat fields north-east of Carlisle. The little church, built in 1854 on the site of a much older one, is dedicated to St. John the Evangelist. The windows on each side are rather unusual. It would be easy not to notice anything special about the memorial to men who fell in the 1914–18 war and which is fixed to the wall beside the door; in fact it is made of oak taken from the cadet training ship *Britannia*, at Dartmouth from 1869 to 1905. Next to the church is the village school, still bearing above its doors the wording 'National School 1844', surmounted by a clock and bell-cote. From the name of the village, a cross must have stood there in ancient times, probably on the little hill where the church is today.

At Houghton, the vicar is separated by the motorway from his pleasant church, built in 1840 and dedicated, like that at Crosby, to St. John the Evangelist. Its altar is at the west end, not the east. Next to it is the old village school, used as such until about fifteen years ago. Added to, it is now the church hall. Between the church and the original village are mainly new houses, for Houghton has become a popular dormitory village for professional and managerial classes working in Carlisle. The former Wesleyan chapel built in 1893 is now a shop (John Wesley slept at Houghton on Good Friday 1770). The village hall beside the green has a clock, erected to commemorate the coronation of Elizabeth II. There is no pub in the village. The name indicates 'a place on a spur of hill'. I have not heard for very many years of the ghost, or boggle, of a woman dressed in white, who is said to have appeared on winters' nights near Houghton church on the road to Brunstock a hundred or so years ago. She is supposed to have drowned herself in a water trough.

On the road to Longtown a few straggling cottages, houses and farms of no particular beauty form the village of Blackford. The church, dedicated to St. John the Baptist, stands away from the rest of the village. It is a plain building erected in 1869 and has been looked after since 1961 by the vicar of Scaleby. Its eagle lectern in oak is of Japanese craftsmanship, according to Bulmer (1901). The undistinguished war memorial to both wars stands just inside the churchyard. The school is next to the church, but Blackford has neither village hall nor pub. At the turn of the century, children at the school above Standard III paid one penny per week to help to support it.

The most northerly village in Cumbria is Penton. It can be reached from Longtown by the road running past Netherby Hall, with its connections with Scott's Young Lochinvar—'So boldly he entered the Netherby Hall' and carried off the bride. This quiet road goes through miles of open fields with beautiful views across to Scotland. Netherby has been lived in for several centuries by the Graham family, and the grounds are open to the public on a Sunday in April for the gathering of daffodils on behalf of charities. Much of the county is golden with wild flowering daffodils at this time of year. Penton is true to the pattern of the very northern villages by straggling over a wide area. The pub, 'The Bridge Inn', is at the crossroads. The store and station lie a short distance away. The station is now disused and the railway lines have been taken up. The church is two miles farther at Nicholforest. It is dedicated to St. Nicholas, and is a pleasant little building rebuilt in 1866–7, with small windows in an apse at the east end.

A village deriving its name from Hadrian's Wall is Walton. It is an attractive place set in open country with fine views to the north-east. 'The Centurion Inn' (formerly 'The Black Bull'), bespeaks of its nearness to the Wall, and a signpost at the Inn indicates a small section of the Wall which can be seen some 500 yards to the east. The village is plentifully served with greens, including the triangular village green in front of the church. St. Mary's church was erected in 1869–70 and has a rather unusual reredos given by the Johnson family in 1899; a large mosaic panel with a vine motive. There is a small Methodist chapel dated 1858, and a reading room (1893), which is now a billiard hall and meeting room.

The most easterly village covered by this chapter is Gilsland, half in Cumberland and half in Northumberland. Its name shows a close link with Bewcastle for 'Gille', whose 'land' it was, was the son of Bueth. The Roman Wall passed close to the village and many remains of it can be seen beside the road which runs westwards to Banks Turret and lovely Lanercost Priory. Gilsland's church, dedicated to St. Mary Magdalene and consecrated in 1854, is up the hill north of the village. A little farther beyond it is a steep path down to a sulphur spring. Gilsland was at one time a very popular spa, and the water from the spring can still be drunk (rather than enjoyed) close to the footbridge over the Irthing river. All this district is full of memories of Sir Walter Scott, the novelist and poet. At the Popping Stones, a little farther upstream from the sulphur spring, he is supposed to have 'popped the question' to Charlotte Carpenter who became his wife on Christmas Eve in 1797 in Carlisle Cathedral. In Gilsland village there is Merrilees Cottage.

Three miles west of Gilsland, and hardly worth a visit for its own sake, is the undistinguished stump, all that remains of the fourteenth-century Triermain Castle. It is a travesty of 'the lordly halls of Triermain' of Scott's 'The Bridal of Triermain'. The Castle is also mentioned in Coleridge's 'Christabel'. A large farm now stands close to it, built probably from its tumbled-down stones. The rocket testing station of Spadeadam can be seen on the sky-line to the north.

Another Scott memory is recalled at Upper Denton. In the churchyard is the gravestone of Margaret Carrick who died in 1717 at Mumps Hall, mentioned in *Guy Mannering*. It is claimed for the arch in this church that it is one of the oldest arches standing in any church. It was transported and rebuilt stone by stone from the Roman Wall at Birdoswald. Denton means 'place in a valley'. Low Row, nearby on the level crossing, is now probably of village status. Its church of St. Cuthbert was built in 1866 on the site of an older one. It has a pub, 'The Railway Inn'; and a village hall, the Taylor Institute, built in 1916. What for many years was Carrick's Dairy, noted for its butter and cheese, is now a small engineering works.

Three villages which lie on the A69 Carlisle–Brampton road complete this chapter. Aglionby, although listed as a village, has no church, no pub, no village hall and no shop. It takes its name from the family who held the manor from shortly after the Norman Conquest until 1785. Their name recurs frequently as Mayor of Carlisle during the fifteenth, sixteenth, seventeenth and eighteenth centuries; the earliest was John Aglionby who was Mayor in 1463. A letter from Lord Scrope dated 26th December 1599 tells of 'a foul murder within two miles of Carlisle the Sunday next to Christmas on the person of an honest gentleman esquire . . . named Edward Aglionby, often maior of Carlel, and ever ready to serve the Quene'. One of the murderers involved was a Graham 'now fled into Scotland'. At the outbreak of Bonnie Prince Charlie's rebellion in 1745 the Mayor was Henry Aglionby, but he is recorded as never appearing within the city during the trouble, leaving everything to his Deputy Mayor. There are a few older houses and farms at Aglionby, but its nearness to Carlisle has resulted in the building of new good class houses. Building is still in progress.

Warwick is separated from its church by the A69. It is a village of attractive old brick-built houses, with much modern building. The pub, 'The Queens Arms', is on the outskirts of the village. It was the first of the nationalized houses to be sold after the State Management Scheme was abolished in 1972. The church of St. Leonard, which Pevsner calls 'the most memorable Norman village church in Cumberland', is along an unsurfaced road which also passes the former Methodist church (1847). Inside St. Leonard's are tablets to members of the Warwick family one of whom, Francis, was 'shot to death', with his wife, by mutineers in India in 1857. The three-arched bridge over the river Eden at the foot of the hill, by the famous John Dobson of Newcastle, was built in 1837. Warwick means the 'dwelling on the bank'. On one side of the river is Warwick Hall and on the other side Holme Eden Hall. The latter was built in 1840, also by John Dobson, for Peter Dixon who had in Carlisle the largest cotton mill in England at the time. He was Mayor of Carlisle in 1837–8. The Hall is now occupied by an enclosed Order of Benedictine nuns. It was at Warwick Bridge that the Jacobite army mustered on 13th November 1745, formed into marching order, and moved forward to attack Carlisle. They carried with them scaling ladders made from branches and young trees gathered in the area. Along this road, too, Bonnie Prince Charlie rode four days later on his white horse to take over the city. The family at Warwick Hall were Roman Catholic, and strong Jacobite sympathizers, and Prince Charles Edward had been entertained at the Hall during his stay in Brampton. After the Scots' final defeat at Culloden they adopted Ranald Macdonald of Tirnadris whose father had been killed in the battle. The present Warwick Hall is not the same building. It was rebuilt in 1828, and then again in 1936, after a serious fire in 1933.

The mixture of old and new that makes up the village of Warwick Bridge is unremarkable. It has three churches—the Roman Catholic one of Our Lady and St. Wilfrid, built by Pugin in 1841; the Anglican church; and the Methodist church, 1908. The pub is 'The George'. Beside it is the Cumberland Mills branch of Otterburn Mills Ltd. The Anglican church of St. Paul is on the outskirts of the village, and is chiefly interesting as having been built entirely at the expense of Peter Dixon, mentioned above, of Holme Eden Hall, in 1840. The church, like the Hall, was built by Dobson of Newcastle. Local opinion has it that Dixon, who worshipped at St. Leonard's church in Warwick, was offended by a sermon preached there and, out of pique, in 1846 employed Dobson to build St. Paul's. There is a monument to him and his wife in the church as well as several other memorial tablets to Dixons, one of whom, Francis Peter Dixon, was four times Mayor of Carlisle between 1883 and 1915. The church tower is 110 feet high.

2

The Vale of Eden

BETWEEN the motorway and the northern Pennines lies some of the loveliest scenery to be found anywhere in England. In it, particularly along the banks of the river Eden, are some of the most delightful villages, and to loiter among its winding lanes can bring a real benison of beauty and serenity. This chapter covers the area south of the A69, Carlisle to Newcastle, and north of the A686, Penrith to Alston, roads.

Great Corby, 'Core's settlement' (the 'by' in this and other Cumbrian villages indicates a Scandinavian link), stands above the Eden on its right bank. It is a much bigger village in fact than it seems to be at first, and has some unusual and very attractive houses. Below the village square is the cottage from which until a few years ago the rowing-boat ferried passengers between Corby and Wetheral on the opposite bank. In the square is the pub, 'The Queen Inn', and an ugly arched building erected in 1833 as a blacksmith's shop, with a covered open space for shoeing the horses. It was intended to represent Vulcan's Forge; Pevsner calls it an exedra. The reading room nearby was built by public subscription in 1877 and has the 1914–18 war memorial tablet beside the door. It is now used as the village hall. There is a Methodist church dated 1889. A school was established as early as 1720. Beside the present school is an unusual pump surmounted by a cross crosslet. It does not work. The lovely grounds of Corby Castle are open to the public each Thursday.

North-eastwards, and unexpectedly close to the A69, is the quiet and wholly delightful village of Hayton. It has public seats made by the boys of the Edmond Castle Reform School, on the other side of the main road. The pub is 'The White Lion'. The church, of St. Mary Magdalene, was built in 1780 on the site of an old church. The tower was raised in 1888 and the three-dial clock installed three years later. On the north side, and from inside the church looking rather like a musicians' gallery, is the Graham pew, with the family vaults underneath. It has its own door from the churchyard. The name Hayton means 'hay farm'. It was at one time the custom there to distribute ale amongst the parishioners three times a year—twelve gallons at Candlemas, twelve gallons at the feast of St. Andrew (30th November), and twenty-four gallons at Easter.

Nestling in the lovely scenery of the northern Pennines, and providing since early this century a reservoir from which Carlisle draws much of its water, is Castle Carrock—the 'fortified castle', although it is not known that one ever existed. Two pubs face each other in this small community—'The Duke of Cumberland' and 'The Weary Sportsman'. Close by is the village hall, the Watson Institute, built in 1897 and modernized in 1959. The present church, dedicated to St. Peter, was rebuilt and enlarged in 1828 and contains much of the fabric of the previous church. Its royal arms are those of Queen Anne. The east window is worth seeing. A wall tablet is in memory of D. Fenwick Steavenson (1844–1920), the County Court Judge. He lived for a time at Gelt Hall and made and presented the litany desk still in use. There is a stone staircase outside the church leading to the belfry.

A number of small villages lie in a curve from Castle Carrock towards the Northumberland border and round the northern end of the Pennines. Talkin is a blue-grey village gathered, though with an air of neglect, round a crossroads. It has two pubs, 'The Hare and Hounds' and 'The Blacksmith's Arms'. The reading room (1898) is now used as the village hall, and is next door to the now disused Wesleyan chapel (1870). The church was built in the middle of the last century but has a Norman pulpit and communion rail. Talkin Tarn nearby is busy in the summer months with swimming, boating and yachting; occasional regattas are held there. Like many inland tarns it has its legend of a submerged city whose ruins may sometimes be seen when the light is in the right direction. Long, long ago a prophet was sent to warn the local inhabitants that God intended to wreak vengeance on them for their wickedness. All but one poor widow ignored him, and the flood which covered the houses stopped short at her cottage.

Close to Talkin Tarn is Farlam, 'a fern clearing'. There is little to say about it. Its church, dedicated to St. Thomas à Becket, and built in 1860, has a short flight of railed steps leading to its pulpit. The war memorial, to the dead of both World Wars and also to those killed in Korea, is in the churchyard. There is a Lowthian Church Hall built in 1928.

Milton, 'the place with a mill', is dominated by one huge farm silo. There is a small Methodist chapel and a pub, 'The New Inn', situated right on the level crossing at Milton Junction, on the Newcastle–Carlisle Railway. This was the first east to west railway in the country, opened in June 1838, and Milton's chief claim to fame is that here began the present railway ticket system. Thomas Edmondson (1792–1851), a Quaker, was the first stationmaster at the small roadside station, which was later re-named Brampton Junction, in 1836. The type of voucher which had been used for coach passengers was being used for rail passengers and was proving inconvenient. Edmondson introduced the small cardboard ticket and invented the ticket printing machine eventually to be adopted all over the world.

Where two side roads join the main Brampton to Alston road, B6292, is Hallbankgate. Its pub is 'The Belted Will', named after Lord William Howard who owned Naworth Castle in Elizabethan times. He is referred to in Scott's *Lay of the Last Minstrel*. The pub regained its licence in only 1968, after being a temperance hotel for eighty years. The village store is the Naworth Collieries Co-operative Industrial Society Ltd., and the two are an indication of the influence of Naworth Castle, a short distance away on the other side of the A69. There is a Wesleyan chapel (1883) and a village hall with, almost opposite, a small smithy where wrought iron is made. Sir Winston Churchill addressed a public meeting in the village in October 1900.

Midgeholme, situated right on the Northumberland border, is nothing but a school (which used to be a church), a telephone kiosk, a few houses, and a row of empty workmen's cottages. It is at the foot of Tindale Fells where good quality coal used to be mined—the last pit closed in 1953. As the mining came to an end the village declined, as also did Tindale itself in a cul-de-sac on the south side of the road. The church of St. Michael is at Tindale. The Wesleyan chapel (1888) has not been used since 1966 and opposite it is a former reading room bearing the same date, but now a farmer's store. What was obviously quite a large co-operative store served what was, as recently as twenty to thirty years ago, a thriving community. Since the mines closed very few of the original villagers remain, but the cottages are being taken over and renovated by townsfolk as weekend homes. The cutting in which ran the coal-carrying railway, built about 1798, can still be seen. George Stephenson's famous *Rocket* ran on this line.

The villages which lie in the Eden valley include a few which are more like fellside villages. Cumwhitton is one of these. Its red sandstone houses and farms would seem to breed good darts players if the number of certificates hanging in 'The Red Lion' are anything to go by. Its small, friendly church, dedicated to St. Mary, celebrated its octocentenary in 1960. It contains Anglo-Saxon and Norman work. Separate war memorials for the 1914–18 and 1939–45 wars are inside the church, together with other memorial plaques. A modern (1962) stained glass window on the north side I found attractive. There is a two-decker pulpit, and the font is dated 1662. A vertical sundial on the south side of the church carries the motto '*Homo quasi umbra*'—'Man is like a shadow' (Psalm 144 v. 4). The western tower has an outside stairway. The clock in it was given in memory of those who served in the 1914–18 war. On the green in front of the church is a Jubilee drinking fountain, 1897. There is a public hall and reading room dated 1901. A few of the houses in the village have to be reached over a small stream which runs alongside the road before going under it. The post office and general store is near the church. The pub is at one end of the village and a disused Wesleyan chapel (1891) at the other end. Robert Robinson, a blacksmith of Cumwhitton, was found guilty, together with his son William, of the manslaughter of a river bailiff on 15th January 1862. They were poaching salmon.

Cumrew, 'the valley by the hill', is obviously a farming community, set in narrow winding lanes with the fells rising above.

The church of St. Mary was rebuilt in 1890; an unusual-looking building, it lies along an unmade-up road. A church has been known here since 1291. The register records that at the time of the Civil Wars 'a great many children of foreigners were baptised here'—presumably a reference to those Scots who came in on the side of Parliament and who, under General Lesley, besieged Carlisle during its longest siege from October 1644 to June 1645. In the church is an effigy of a lady with a puppy by her pillow, most probably representing Joan Dacre who died in 1324. Near the church is a lovely 1753 house with some excellent topiary. There is now no pub and no shop in the village although at the beginning of this century there were two pubs, 'The Rising Sun' and 'The Seven Stars'.

Still skirting the Pennines the way leads to Croglin, on the swiftly flowing river of that name. Wordsworth wrote:

> Down from the Pennine Alps, how fiercely sweeps
> Croglin, the stately Eden's tributary!

The name comes from the words for 'bend' and 'torrent'. The village was burned by the Scots in May 1346. It has had a church since Norman times, and its rectors can be named since 1294. The present church, to St. John the Baptist, was rebuilt in 1878. Outside it is the tomb of Robert, the Bishop of Carlisle who died in 1278. Opposite the church is an old rectory pele-tower. The 1914–18 war memorial is just outside the church door. The pub is 'The Robin Hood Inn' and down the road from it is the wooden hut which serves as a village hall. In a quarry beyond the church was found, in 1883, a mould for making spearheads, probably dating back to about 2000 B.C. It was Croglin Watty who, in the dialect poem by Cumberland's bard Robert Anderson, was hired at Carlisle Fair by the Carlisle miser Margery Jackson. The most famous story connected with Croglin is, of course, that of the Croglin Vampire. It appears in Augustus Hare's *The Story of my life* and purports to have been told by Captain Fisher, whose family owned Croglin Grange. The house was let to two brothers and a sister who were excellent tenants. One summer night the sister was attacked by a creature with 'a hideous brown face with flaming eyes' which got into her room and bit her in the throat.

The famous carvings on Bewcastle Cross have withstood 1,300 years of wild weather across the fells

The 1828 Methodist chapel at Scaleby Hill

The 'Popping Stones' near Gilsland, where Sir Walter Scott proposed to Charlotte Carpenter in 1797

The village of Warwick Bridge

'The Duke of Cumberland' inn at Castle Carrock

The church and village of Croglin

Gamblesby, where John Wesley built a chapel in 1784

She screamed, and the creature fled. The three went to Switzerland while she recovered but returned later to Croglin. The following March the creature again appeared at her window. One of the brothers managed to shoot it in the leg as it fled, but it scrambled over the churchyard wall and disappeared into a family vault. The vault was opened next day and the contents of the many coffins were discovered, horribly mangled and distorted, scattered over the floor. Only one coffin remained intact, and it, as might be expected, held the brown, withered, shrivelled, mummified and hideous figure with the marks of a recent pistol shot in one leg.

Only Augustus Hare records the strange tale of the Croglin Vampire, and no Croglin Grange ever stood near the churchyard wall, but there is a true story of a great bat connected with the next village along the Pennine foothills. When the old church at Renwick was being rebuilt in 1733 an enormous bat flew out of the ruins and scared the villagers. One, bolder than the rest, urged the others to return with him armed with sticks, and the monster was killed. The brave man was suitably rewarded; but the natives are still referred to as 'Renwick Bats'. The original church was almost certainly founded by the Celtic missionaries before A.D. 600 and burnt and ravaged during the border wars and the struggles with the reivers. The present church, dedicated to All Saints, was built in 1845. It has the two-decker pulpit from the old church. There is also a Methodist church, originally built in 1818 but repaired, and a school added, in 1863. The name Renwick is a contraction of Ravenswick, and indicates a position near the banks of the Raven beck. I was rather surprised to see in so apparently remote a spot a craft and coffee shop.

The most southerly of the fell-side villages covered by this chapter is Gamblesby—'the land of Gamel (son of Bern)'. It is a spacious village mainly of red sandstone houses and farms, with quite a number of mid-eighteenth century houses. 'The Red Lion' carries the date 1741 above its door. The village stocks are still to be seen at the junction with the Glassonby road. They are iron shackles rather than the traditional wooden type with holes. The church, of St. John the Evangelist, was built in 1868. Its east end is an apse. The Wesleyan chapel of 1864 replaced an older one said to have been designed and built by John Wesley himself in 1784. He preached twice in Gamblesby, in April 1751 and in May 1780. There is also a Congregational chapel dated 1864. The post office is a private house. The village school closed in 1970 and the building has been converted by the villagers themselves into a modern community centre which was opened in June 1972.

Just to the south of the A69 lies the straggling village of Scotby. It comprises for the most part new and very new houses. Situated close to the major source of employment, the city of Carlisle, it has obviously become a village taken over by outsiders who have come to it purely because of its convenience to them, not to take part in any of its village life. Some aspect of its original identity lingers round the village green, with the new village hall and, opposite, the pub, 'The Royal Oak'. The village certainly dates back to 1236 and its name indicates a 'settlement of the Scots'. The post office is a private house between the village hall and the church. The church was built in 1854 and squats pleasantly on top of a small hill. Dedicated to All Saints, it is a plain, school-room type of church. Most of its windows are clear glass. Almost everything in it seems to be in memory of someone—including the 1901 pulpit and the great majority of the new-looking pews. The memorial to those who fell in the two world wars is a tall cross at the entrance to the churchyard. The church tower has been inserted rather oddly in the south-east corner of the church. Scotby has had a strong cricketing tradition since 1897. The houses across the road from the green were awarded the Ministry of Housing and Local Government Award for Good Design in 1968. In a garden in the village is preserved Carlisle's last working tram-car.

Pleasant open fields lie between Scotby and Wetheral, often called 'the loveliest village in Cumberland'. I would accept the statement as meaning the village with the loveliest setting in Cumberland. Approached from Scotby the first building in Wetheral is the Methodist church (1873)—tucked away on the very fringe of the village almost as though Methodism were afraid to enter into the community. Like Scotby, Wetheral has almost lost its nature by becoming a dormitory village to Carlisle. The triangular village green, however, despite one or two incongruous large houses, still reveals something of the earlier village's character. This green was one of the last pieces of waste land to be disposed of under the Inglewood Forest Enclosure Act, and was bought for the village for £60 in 1808. The stone cross at the south end replaced the old maypole which formerly stood on the identical steps, but nearer the centre of the green. The steps were moved so that they would interfere less with the children's games. From the green a road leads down quite steeply to the church and the river. The church, dedicated to the Holy Trinity and St. Constantine, is entered under a modern lych-type gate erected to mark the fallen of the parish in the two world wars. In the church itself are two alabaster effigies, of Sir Richard Salkeld and his wife Jane. The Howard chapel, added to the north-east corner of the church, contains what is looked on as one of Nollekens'[1] most important sculptures. With the exception of a tablet in Carlisle Cathedral it is the only work by him in the entire area. Commemorating Lady Maria Howard who died in 1789 one year after her marriage, it shows the young dying woman with her dead baby in her lap, supported by a draped figure pointing upwards. Wordsworth was so moved by this sculpture that he wrote:

> Stretched on the dying mother's lap, lies dead
> Her new-born babe; dire ending of bright hope!

Wetheral is also known for its fishing and its walks. The river Eden runs at the bottom of the hill by the church and is spanned by the Newcastle–Carlisle railway on a viaduct of five eighty-foot arches a hundred feet high. On the opposite bank is the white cottage from which the ferry boat operated until a few years ago. A most delightful walk leads along the Eden, with fine views across to Corby Castle, through Wetheral woods, now National Trust property, to St. Constantine's cells. These three cells are approached today through one very narrow door and, before it and the steps were made, must have been very difficult of access. They are by tradition the cells where the Scottish St. Constantine spent his time as a hermit, and must also have been used over the centuries by refugees from religious and other persecutions, and from justice. Inevitably their walls are now a mass of graffiti carved and scribbled by those with no other claim on posterity. An alternative road

[1] Joseph Nollekens, the sculptor, was born in Soho in 1837.

back to the village passes the gatehouse of the Benedictine Priory founded in 1088. All that now remains of it, the gateway forms part of some farm buildings. The glass in the west end of Wetheral Church came from the Priory; one of the figures depicted is St. Constantine. Wetheral has two pubs, 'The Crown Hotel', well-known to fishermen, and, in the village proper, 'The Wheatsheaf Inn'. Near the 'Wheatsheaf' is the village hall (1891), with its public clock, and the school.

The few solidly built farms and houses, with a sprinkling of new houses, that make up Cumwhinton hardly constitute a village. There is a Methodist Free Church (1904) and at the opposite end of the village the post office and shop. The pub, 'The Lowther Arms', is on the Scotby road. The rather bleak-looking memorial to those who fell in both wars is beside St. John's Hall (1908). St. John's church is in Cotehill, a village perched, as its name suggests, on a hill. It is an unbalanced mixture of the old, almost tumbling down, and the new. One old cottage dated 1698 is set incongruously amongst very new neighbours. Many houses have fairly obviously been built to accommodate workers at the nearby works of British Gypsum Ltd. There is a post office-shop, and a large, ugly village hall (1930), standing on its own; the slab seats in front of it are in memory of Norman Fletcher of Armathwaite. The simple church, of St. John the Evangelist, was built in 1868. It is entered under a lych gate and has an odd, almost Eastern, tower at the north-east corner. I found its unusual east window rather attractive. There is a simple cross to the fallen in the two wars in the churchyard. The village pub is 'The Greyhound Inn'.

The beautiful village of Armathwaite nestles in its wooded hollow beside the river Eden, renowned all around for its salmon fishing. The name Armathwaite means 'the clearing of the hermit'; in summer the village can hardly be seen amongst its trees from a short distance away. The few houses cluster near the attractive bridge and there are lovely walks beside the river. The whole atmosphere of the place is peaceful and serene. The famous Nunnery Walks are only about three miles upstream. It possesses two pubs, an indication of its popularity with anglers, 'The Duke's Head' and, on the other side of the bridge, 'The Red Lion'. The post office-shop is next door but one to a new foodstore. The Women's Institute, founded in 1922, have built their own hall. Armathwaite Castle by the river has recent additions and is now let as apartments. The railway line passes close above the village. To me the great joy of the place is the truly delightful little chapel of Christ and Mary, built before 1668. It is difficult to believe that at one time it was in such a sorry state that it was used as a cattle shed.

East of the Eden and towards Croglin is Ainstable—'the slope overgrown with bracken'. It is not much of a village. Its post office-shop is at the crossroads. The pub, 'The Crown Inn', is almost opposite the Old Forge with its interesting nameplate. Beyond is the village school. The Wesleyan chapel (1861) stands a little aloof, away from the village itself, while the church of St. Michael commands a prominent position on top of a hill, looking down on the village and on miles of surrounding countryside with Saddleback silhouetted on the skyline to the south-west. The churchyard is entered under a war memorial lych gate. The church was rebuilt in 1871–2 and the unattractive tower set into the north-west corner gives a very unusual entrance. In the sanctuary, near the altar, are stone effigies of William Denton and his wife Katherine who died in the early part of the fifteenth century. The effigies used to be in St. Cuthbert's church, Carlisle, before it was rebuilt, and were later at Nunnery before being transferred to Ainstable church. A man born at Ainstable in 1729 was destined to join the ranks of the few Cumbrians to be buried in Westminster Abbey. He was John Leake (1729–1792), 'the man midwife'. He wrote many books on childbirth and women's diseases and founded the Westminster Lying-in Hospital near Westminster Bridge.

Ruckcroft is listed as a village. There are wonderful views from it, but it comprises only a few houses and farms, as does Staffield where there is one house dated 1702. The road from there drops into Kirkoswald, several times winner of the Best Kept Village competition. It has a sort of central square on which are two pubs facing each other, 'The Crown Inn' and 'The Black Bull', the post office, the Church Institute (1910), and the local Women's Institute building. The war memorial stands inside a railed enclosure in the centre. There are several early eighteenth-century houses. The village has cause to be proud of its appearance and villagers have long complained about the electricity and telephone cables criss-crossing the street like cobwebs on the ceiling of some houseproud lady's sitting-room. In 1972 the powers that be agreed to re-route these cables underground at a cost of £12,000.

As long ago as A.D. 1200 Kirkoswald possessed a charter to hold a market each Thursday, and also a fair on the feast of St. Oswald (5th August) each year. Both have been obsolete for very many years now. Horse and pony races and a varied programme of other sports used to be held on Easter Monday. There is a report in 1829 which tells that 'the sports commenced as usual by the catching of a cock with the mouth, which afforded glorious fun to the Johnnies'. The village takes its name from the church of St. Oswald. The church is built at the foot of a hill below the village, and an unusual feature is that its bells ring from a completely separate tower built on top of the hill behind the church and 200 yards away from it, so that they can be heard clearly by the people living to the east. The present bell-tower was built in 1897, replacing a wooden one. The first Christian church on the site was consecrated by St. Aidan in the seventh century. He was accompanied by King Oswald, and they converted to Christianity the people who were at that time worshipping the spring or well. The church was built over it, and it can still be seen outside the west window. The first stone church was built about 1130. In 1523 the church became collegiate and a community of working parish clergy lived at the college opposite until the Dissolution.[1] The college is now lived in by members of the Fetherstonhaugh family who first took up residence in Kirkoswald towards the end of the sixteenth century. One member, Sir Timothy, was an ardent Royalist and thereby incurred the anger of Cromwell who had him beheaded at Chester in 1651. The name Timothy is kept in the family.

Not far away, on the other side of the Eden, is Lazonby, 'the freedman's settlement'. It is a large village with, unexpectedly, a fire station. The people built their own open-air swimming pool in 1964 to the great joy of the children. The school with its odd

[1] The suppression of monasteries by Henry VIII in the sixteenth century.

tower is nearby. The pub is 'The Midland Hotel', close to the railway line. There is a Methodist church (1850) and a library, started in 1858; the books were kept in the Wesleyan school until the reading room was established in 1866. It was extended in 1928. The dedication of the church to St. Nicholas is mildly surprising as he is the patron saint of sailors; it is built on a hill and the present church, consecrated in 1863, took the place of a much older one which had been frequently restored. Its register, dating back to 1537, is the oldest in the diocese. The church contains rather an inordinate amount of wood carving, not all of it of very high quality. By the quantity it must have been a life's work—it was done by a former incumbent, Canon B. W. Wilson, who died in 1921. The churchyard is more interesting. It contains an ancient cross-shaft said to be 800 years old; a very impressive war memorial, behind railings, beside the path up to the church gate; and a tombstone with what may be interpreted as a striking anatomical message—'Let your loins be girded about, and your lights burning. . . .' Lazonby stone, a quartzite sandstone from Lazonby Fell, was at one time much used for pavements and flagging. Most of Carlisle's pavements were of this material, and it was used for the steps at the main entrance to Liverpool's new Anglican cathedral.

There are two Salkelds—Great and Little. They are now separated from each other by the Eden, which can be crossed only at Lazonby to the north or Langwathby to the south. A bridge which at one time spanned the river near Great Salkeld was carried away by a flood in 1360. The Bishop at the time, Bishop Walton, granted each and every sinner in the diocese who should contribute to its repair an indulgence of forty days.

The lovely village of Great Salkeld is west of the river Eden. Its houses of red sandstone blend naturally into the beautiful scenery around. It is a worthy holder of the Best Kept Village award. A Free School was founded in the village before the Reformation. The present school was erected in 1856 and enlarged in 1906; let into the school wall are three lintels all dated 1686. The village hall is dated 1895. The pub, a very welcoming one, has the rather unusual name of 'The Highland Drove'. It was formerly 'The Drovers' Arms'. The post office is a private cottage dated

1854. There is a grocer's shop at one end of the village, and the village store up a steep flight of steps at the other. The main feature of the village, however, is its church—another traditional resting place of St. Cuthbert's body. The massive fourteenth-century tower was designed, like those at Newton Arlosh and Burgh-by-Sands, as a safe refuge from the Scots. It is entered by a wonderful old door in the west wall of the nave, and has a fireplace on the first floor. There is a Roman altar in the church porch, and the Norman doorway into the church is probably the finest in Cumberland. A window in the nave shows St. Cuthbert, and scenes from his life. Another shows the famous William Nicolson (1655–1727), Bishop of Carlisle. Hanging over the vestry door is a breast-plate, helmet and sword. Edward Law (1750–1818), later Lord Ellenborough, who achieved fame by his defence of Warren Hastings and later became Lord Chief Justice of England, was born in the rectory. He was educated at Great Blencow. The memorial to those who fell in both world wars is in the churchyard. The name Great Salkeld means 'a large sallow wood'. A farm south-west of the village, Wolfa, is said to have been held in former times on the payment of a certain number of wolves' heads.

At Little Salkeld, on the other side of the river, there is nothing now worth calling a village. A small chapel, which was formerly used as a barn, is now unused and empty. Salkeld Hall opposite was formerly the residence of the Salkeld family. The owner at the time of the Civil Wars, George Salkeld, was a Royalist and was forced to part with his ancestral home for a trifling consideration to a Cromwellian general. A short distance north of the village stands the ancient stone circle, said to be next to Stonehenge in size, known as Long Meg and her Daughters. Long Meg herself is about eighteen feet high and carries cup and ring carvings. Wordsworth visited the circle and describes his feelings:

> A weight of awe, not easy to be borne
> Fell suddenly upon my spirit—cast
> From the dread bosom of the unknown past,
> When first I saw that family forlorn.

Langwathby, 'the settlement at the long ford', is on the east bank of the Eden. The bridge which crossed the river was washed away in the flood of 1968 and has been replaced by a one-way only metal girder bridge. The village surrounds its large green with at one end the village hall, and at the other 'The Shepherds Inn'. The church, of St. Peter, was built by the parishioners in 1718 on the site of an old one. A new porch was added in 1836 and a new east window was provided with other alterations in 1883. In the church are pieces of seventeenth-century armour; probably the equipment of the local militia, and an example of the kind used by most villages of these parts in former days. A tablet tells of the gift of £21, left in 1703 for 'ye releife of ye poor of Langwathby'. An unusual roll of honour of Langwathby School is in the church porch; it bears the actual photographs of the men who served in the 1914–18 war. There is a post office-village store; one house is dated 1699. The Wesleyan church (1860) is near the railway station. There is mention in 1612 of horse races at Langwathby, and racing on Langwathby Moor is referred to in 1700. H. de Vere Stacpoole, the author of the famous best-seller *The Blue Lagoon* spent some time in the village as locum for the doctor.

Grey, drab Hunsonby, 'the settlement of the dog keepers', has little to commend it. There is a Methodist church, and a small open-air swimming pool near the school. The school has a bell-cote with a bell. Nearby Winskill, 'the shelter against the wind', has a Sons of Temperance room.

A village set in lovely, wooded countryside, and with one or two particularly beautiful gardens, is Glassonby, 'Glassan's settlement'. Its church, dedicated to St. Michael, is set peacefully away from the village behind a clump of trees. It is known as Addingham Church, although there is now no such place—it was washed away in floods when the Eden changed its course. The old church stood much closer to the east bank of the river but was desecrated by the spilling of blood in 1360, and the vicar was allowed to officiate in his own house. The present church is probably fifteenth-century and contains items from the earlier church, including pieces of a ninth-century cross in the porch and a hogback gravestone. Vicars can be traced back to the thirteenth century. Two notable ones were William Nicolson (1655–1727), who was vicar previous to his elevation to bishop; and Dr. William Paley (1743–1805), the eminent theological writer and thinker. There is a pitch pipe[1] in a glass case by the chancel arch. The memorial tablet in the church to the fallen of the 1914–18 war covers the men of Glassonby, Gamblesby, Little Salkeld, and Hunsonby and Winskill. The Wesleyan chapel (1869) continues as a Methodist church.

Before the coming of the motorway, the A6 was noisy with a never-ending stream of fast moving cars and lorries. Now it is peaceful. The pleasant village of High Hesket is skirted by it. The name stands for 'the high race-course', although I know of no record of races held there. It comprises one long main street with harmonious houses and bungalows on each side. The church, of St. Mary, is next to 'The Salutation Inn'. One entry to the churchyard is by an unusual little iron wicket up some steps, and the war memorial is just inside the churchyard. Steps outside the church lead up to the belfry; a small bell turret carries two bells. Inside the church the royal coat of arms dated 1856 hangs prominently above the door. The low chancel looks particularly attractive as one enters. A memorial tablet to Bernard Kirkbride, twice High Sheriff of Cumberland and a Lieutenant-Colonel in Charles I's army, is dated 1677. A fine view of the northern Pennines from the back of the church is marred by electricity pylons.

Tradition has it that a chapel was first erected on this spot in 1530 when the plague was ravishing the area. People were bringing their dead as usual to be buried inside the city of Carlisle. The mayor and citizens would not permit them to enter the city gates but, from its walls, advised them to bury the corpses at a place then called Walling Stone, promising that if they did so they would ask the Bishop to consecrate a chapel there.

Near High Hesket was at one time Castle Hewen or, according to Leland, Castle Lewen. An old ballad tells of a knight who dwelt in this castle in the days when King Arthur and Queen Guinevere lived 'in merrie Carlisle'. He was:

Twyce the size of common men,
Wi' thewes and sinewes stronge,
And on his back he bears a clubbe
That is both thick and longe.

[1] A small pipe to pitch the voice or tune.

After a complaint about him King Arthur went out to tame the miscreant, but was bewitched, and only allowed to go free on the condition that he would return next New Year's Day with an answer to the question: 'What is it that woman loveth best?' He sought the answer in vain until one day he met an old hag who gave him the information—"woman loveth her own will best"—for his promise to marry her to some gallant knight. Sir Gawain agreed to marry her, and her own spell being broken she was transformed into the fairest of the fair. Another legend has it that a man of gigantic stature who lived in the castle was buried in Penrith churchyard, in what is today known as the 'Giant's Grave'; which was maybe the genesis of James Joyce's book *Finnegan's Wake*.

At the crest of a hill on the west side of the main A6 road between High Hesket and Low Hesket may still be seen, out of line with the rest of the hedge, a thorn tree growing through a stone platform. This is the traditional Court Thorn, beneath whose branches tenants assembled at the manorial court to pay their feudal dues each year on the feast of St. Barnabas (11th June). A little farther north, on Wragmire Moss, there stood the last tree of the great Inglewood Forest which once extended from Carlisle to Penrith. The tree was, for six hundred years, a recorded boundary mark between the parishes of High Hesket and St. Mary's, Carlisle. It fell from sheer old age, said to be almost one thousand years old, on 13th June 1823.

Between the A6 and the motorway, and so close to it that the hum of its ceaseless traffic can be heard from the village green, is one of the most delightful villages I know. Its name, Wreay, means 'a remote, or isolated, place' and although only five miles from Carlisle this description almost applies to it today. Lovely peaceful views can be seen all around it. It is full of interesting stories, and has probably the most unusual and fascinating church in Cumberland. It still has its village parliament, the 'Twelve Men of Wreay', which was founded almost three hundred years ago; the only qualification for its members is that they must live in the parish. From about 1780 to 1880 Wreay had its own mayor elected annually, sometimes from the village, sometimes from Carlisle. Every Shrove Tuesday from 1655 until 1790 cockfighting took place on the village green, the winner holding for a year a silver bell engraved 'Wrey Chapple 1655'. Cockfighting was superseded by a hunt of harriers which continued until 1880; but the bell was stolen in 1872. A lime tree was planted on the village green in 1897 to commemorate the Diamond Jubilee of Queen Victoria. The pub is 'The Plough Inn'.

A school was built about 1760 but was already ruinous in 1830 when it was replaced by orders of a Miss Sarah Losh, a well-known local resident. The school was enlarged in 1906; near it is a handsome village hall. A chapel dedicated to St. Mary is known to have existed in Wreay from 1319. It was improved in 1739 and its font, dated 1738, may still be seen in the churchyard. By 1840 the chapel was in a very dilapidated condition and Miss Losh, who had already rebuilt the school, agreed to defray the cost of erecting a new church, to the south of the old one, provided she was left unrestricted as to its design and building. She was her own architect and designed every detail, the work being carried out by village masons and builders. Sarah Losh (1786–1853) had travelled widely and the Italian influence is very noticeable in her church, which is much more attractive inside than out. The main windows seem to be made up of small pieces taken from other windows, but give a quite beautiful effect. The small windows all round the church are equally unusual and effective. It is, however, the carvings everywhere which are the most striking. They should be seen rather than described—animals, insects and plants abound; tortoises, alligators, beetles, butterflies, water-lilies, eagles, a pelican, a bat—the list is long. The pulpit is made from the hollow trunk of bog oak with a palm tree beside it to hold a candle; the alabaster font was carved by Miss Losh herself; the west door carving was done by her gardener, and represents a gourd-plant with a caterpillar eating at the base of the stem; the altar is of green marble from Italy. Pine-cones and arrows form a recurring motive, and are connected with a Major William Thain, a former pupil of Wreay School who was killed on the Khyber Pass by a poisoned arrow. The pine-cone was for Miss Losh the emblem of life after death. In a corner of the churchyard is the Losh family burial enclosure, with a copy of the Bewcastle Cross erected in memory of Sarah's parents and near it a mausoleum containing an alabaster carving of Sarah's beloved sister Katherine who died in 1835. The figure is the work of David Dunbar who had a studio in Carlisle. Sarah is said to have stood over him to make sure that the likeness was a good one. The villagers and school children planted two lime trees in April 1853—one between the church and the vicarage in memory of Sarah Losh, and one south of the church in memory of Katherine. The house in which Sarah Losh had lived, Woodside, was bought early this century by Mr Andrew Gibson, a wealthy Liverpool shipowner. He had intended to move into it in 1912 but his wife died just before the removal and he could not bear to live in it nor to permit anyone else to do so. Wreay Woods were bought by a Yorkshire timber firm in 1965 and most of the trees were felled, but they are now being replanted.

3

East and North-east of Penrith

THIS chapter concerns itself with the villages contained in the triangle bound by the A686 to Alston, the Pennines, and the A66 from Penrith to Stainmore. Most of them are Westmorland villages, and most lie to the east of the lovely river Eden, between it and the foothills of the Pennines. Four, however, stand grimly high in the bleak moorlands to the far east and look down on their fellows in the softer lowlands. The Penrith–Alston road is the first to be blocked by the snows of winter, and the last to be re-opened. The road over Stainmore is the way the Romans came; was for centuries one of the few links between Cumberland and the rest of England; and has many tales to tell of travellers, and in more modern times lorries, caught in the snowdrifts and benighted.

Nenthall and Nenthead stand apart on the Alston moors near the eastern boundary of Cumberland. At a bend in the Alston–Nenthead road is the war memorial to the men of Nenthall who gave their lives for their country. A little farther along is the Wesleyan chapel, built in 1823. Wesleyanism held a strong appeal for the sturdy, independent folk of the remote dales. Nearby, a telephone kiosk and a sprinkling of houses and farms make up the village. The pub, 'The Horse and Waggon', is set back slightly from the road. Next to it is a house dated 1700. On the outskirts of Nenthead is a house with a weathervane in the form of a man apparently shooting a goose. The fellsides around are honeycombed with old lead workings, and the County Council has recently completed a 'clearance of dereliction' operation on the mine wastes. They are still ugly, but time may bring some softness to them. Nenthead itself was built as a model village in the early nineteenth century by the London Lead Company. It was prosperous then, and lead, zinc and copper ore were worked. As recently as the beginning of this century 2,000 tons of ore were exported annually to Belgium. The mines have been closed since 1919, apart from a very short re-opening about 1926. Some of the slag heaps were worked during and just after the war. John Smeaton, the Yorkshireman of Eddystone Lighthouse fame, constructed an underground waterway four miles in length from the Nenthead mines to Alston. At the main crossroads there is still the fountain given in 1877 by the London Lead Company, and the former Lead Company's workmen's reading room is now an 'Over Sixty' club.

The old school built by the Mining Company in 1864 still dominates a hill above the village, but was replaced in 1899. Near the fountain is the store, the post office, the Wesleyan church (1873) and a house dated 1760. The plain, rather bleak, Church of St. John was built in 1845 on a site presented by the London Lead Company. It was 'beautified' in 1876, and an organ was added in 1880. It has an unusual bell turret, and inside is the roll of honour to the men who died in both world wars. Nenthead claims to have the highest house, the highest vicarage, and the highest parish church in the whole of England.

A steep road leads from Nenthead to Garrigill, formerly known as Gerrard's Gill. It is a little gem of a village grouped round its village green. By the river are two mounds of earth known as High and Low Butt Hill, about seventy yards apart, where archery used to be practised. Not far away is the Primitive Methodist Chapel dated 1885. At the other end of the village is the small Redwing Congregational chapel, 1757. An annual service is still held there. Round the green are the post office and store, a second store, and 'The George and Dragon' hotel with the inscription *quo fata vocant* (wherever fate may call) on its sign. There is a house dated 1750 and a building bearing a plaque 'Girls' School built 1850'. The church, dedicated to St. John, was built in 1790 on the site of an early chapel. Bulmer comments that it is 'devoid of every architectural beauty' but I cannot entirely agree with him. It contains the roll of honour; a holy water stoup discovered in

1908; and a rough old font which was reinstated in 1899 after being buried for many years.

There is little to see of the most easterly village in Cumbria, but most travellers have heard of Stainmore. Sir Daniel Fleming, writing in 1671, describes 'that high, hilly and solitary country, exposed to wind and rain, which, because it is stony, is called in our native language Stanemoor, over which is a great but no good road . . . coaches going often that way, though with some difficulty and hazard of overturning and breaking'. North Stainmore today is no more than a few houses and scattered farms, a deserted church, a telephone kiosk beside the A66, a Methodist church dated 1868, and the former coaching house, 'The Punch Bowl Hotel'. The church of St. Mary opposite the hotel was built in 1860–1 but was declared redundant in 1972.

To return to the villages along the Eden, just south of the A686 is Edenhall; from the road one sees the magnificent cricket pavilion opened in May 1972 at a cost of £4,000. The village itself is not particularly noteworthy, its principal features being its church and its 'Luck'. According to a writer in 1791, it was the custom for the young people of the neighbourhood to assemble at the Giant's Caves (near the farm called Honeypot) on the third Sunday in May. They would drink a sweet drink provided by the girls; the day was called 'Sugar and Water Sunday'. Afterwards they adjourned to the pub for a different kind of drink provided by the young men. Sadly, no young people to whom I spoke had heard of 'Sugar and Water Sunday'. The history of the village is closely linked with that of the Musgrave family, who claimed descent from a knight who came over with William the Conqueror. The war memorial beside the road carries the name of Christopher Musgrave aged fifteen who was killed on 1st November 1914, and most of the memorial tablets in the church are to various members of the Musgrave family. One is to Marie who 'dyed in childbed at Carlisle Castle' in 1664, aged twenty-five. The church, which is very well worth visiting, is set apart from the village in open fields, surrounded by glorious country. Also dedicated to St. Cuthbert, it certainly dates back to the fourteenth century, or earlier. It has a solid oak gallery in the west end, and according to Bulmer its east window is of Venetian work. Within the altar rail is a

The entrance to St Constantine's Cells at Wetheral, called the loveliest village in Cumberland

Kirkoswald village and war memorial

Culgaith. Through the hill below is a railway tunnel 660 yards long

Wreay, a village with a beautiful and unusual church

Milburn village, showing the maypole

Dufton village with its fountain

marble slab inlaid with two brass plates showing a warrior and, very much smaller, his wife. The knight is Sir William Stapleton who died about the middle of the fifteenth century. Also in the church are the original tongues, or clappers, belonging to the bells—the earliest being dedicated to St. Cuthbert, 1380–1420. The 'Luck of Edenhall' is a thirteenth century Syrian glass goblet now in the Victoria and Albert Museum. It was probably brought home by a Musgrave who accompanied King Richard on the Crusades. Legend, however, has it that it was seized by a butler at the Hall who found fairies dancing round it on the lawn. The fairies warned him that:

> Whene'er this cup shall break or fall,
> Farewell the luck of Edenhall.

The cup survives; the Hall does not. It was demolished in 1934. Longfellow uses the legend in his poem translated from the German of Johann Uhland:

> As the goblet ringing flies apart,
> Suddenly cracks the vaulted hall;
> And through the rift the wild flames start;
> The guests in dust are scattered all,
> With the breaking Luck of Edenhall!

At the visitation of the plague in 1598 one quarter of the inhabitants of Edenhall died.

Nearby Culgaith, a long, straggling village, used to be famous for three things—'T' Pea'; Atkisson's sausage; and its brass band. The brass band is long ago defunct. Atkisson's sausage, although still called Culgaith sausage, is not made in the village any longer, although I noticed a lot of pigs about. 'T' Pea' is the hill at the bottom of the village through which the railway passes by means of a tunnel 660 yards long. The pub is 'The Black Swan'. A free school was founded in the village in 1775. There is a Wesleyan Methodist chapel dated 1830 and still in use. The Victoria Institute (1897) is opposite the war memorial. The church of All Saints is a plain but interesting cruciform one, dated 1756 and built on the site of an older church pulled down in that year. It is unusual for so old a church to have no stained glass window. A tablet in the church is to Daniel Dover who died in 1787 and left £60. The interest from this sum was to buy 'bread to be distributed weekly, for ever, amongst such of the poor . . . as shall frequent divine service'. This would seem to be one way of encouraging people to go to church! There is a roll of honour inside the church. In the churchyard is a broken sundial, by Cole of London.

The village of Skirwith straggles along both sides of a ravine cut by Skirwith Beck. 'The Sun Inn' stands beside the bridge over the Beck, with the post office and a general store nearby. The church lies a short way up the stream on its southern side, with the Wesleyan chapel (1868) on the opposite bank. The church, dedicated to St. John the Evangelist and built in 1856, has, according to Bulmer, 'been the theme of universal admiration'. The quaint spire is said to be built so, to withstand the howling Helm winds. All round the church, beside the windows, are carved faces, and this theme is continued inside, round the ornately carved pulpit. Unlike the usual evangelistic church, it has decorative curving brass candlesticks hinged on to the choir stalls, and a crucifix hanging inside the chancel arch. Immediately catching the eye is a highly ornate, gilded chandelier. The chancel steps are of Kilkenny marble, and the chancel itself is tiled. The Lady chapel in the south aisle is dedicated to Lieut. T. C. Parker, killed in 1917.

Most of the village of Melmerby is set away from the main road behind the village green. It is a pleasant village with many trees, a great number of them deliberately planted to act as a wind-break against the Helm wind. Here the road to Alston begins to climb and a notice at the edge of the village reads 'winter conditions can be dangerous'. At Hartside, 1,903 feet, is the first road blocked by snow, always, and the last to be cleared. 'The Shepherds Inn' is dated 1789. The general store is next door. Above the green, the village school, 1862, looks rather like a church. There is a village hall. The small, plain church lies slightly away from the village; its east window gives a lop-sided look to that end. Its battlemented tower has a stepped turret. An obelisk memorial just inside the churchyard is to those who fell for their country. Carved heads of a king and a queen adorn either side of the porch. The dedication is to St. John the Baptist; inside, the striking feature is the large east window of plain glass permitting, rather like that at Barbon, a view of the fells. The pews are coated with a nasty thick varnish. Two ancient windows in the north wall were re-opened in 1928. Three coats of arms, all similar, hang on the walls and carry the motto *Pie repone te*—(In pious confidence).

Ousby, 'Ulf's settlement', comprises scattered groups of houses with little unity to them, although they are for the most part set along a triangle of roads. The pub, 'The Fox Inn', stands alone at one end. There is a Wesleyan chapel of 1838 with additions made in 1872, and a village hall, 1858. It is, however, as so often in these villages, in the church where the real interest lies. Dedicated to St. Luke it is isolated from the village, out by Ousby Town Head in the quiet seclusion of fields and is reached along a road that stops at the nearby farms. It is a plain stone building, restored and almost entirely rebuilt in 1858. It has a twin bell-cote, with bells. Above the altar is a stained glass window of St. Luke. The war memorial to 1914–18 is in the sanctuary. Its rectors are known back to 1214, and amongst them is Thomas Robinson, rector from 1672 to 1719, who published material on the natural history of Cumberland and Westmorland. The long, narrow church contains one of the very few carved oak figures of the thirteenth, or early fourteenth, century in existence, for oak was not much used at that time. This figure has survived an unknown number of years buried in the ground, and doubtless also vandalism from ignorant people. It is the almost life-size effigy of a knight with crossed legs and feet resting on his dog. His coat of mail can still be plainly distinguished, and a short dagger hangs from his belt. Some rather poor verse in the church porch tells how:

In Ousby Church near Ardale Rill
A knight in oak rests on his sill.
Awakened from his sleep by plough
Why buried so—one knows not how.

It is most likely that he was a crusader, but Bishop Nicolson speaks of the local tradition that he was an outlaw who lived at Crewgarth, a little over a mile away, and was killed while he was hunting on the mountain above Ousby.

Kirkland is a very small, out-of-the-way place with little of merit except its church and its surrounding countryside. Its name in fact stands for 'land belonging to the church'. The church is dedicated to St. Lawrence the Martyr, and is of ancient foundation. Outside it looks rather neglected. One window beside the porch is repaired with rusty corrugated iron, and the wide grass path to its door shows little sign of wear. The bells in its twin bell-cote are rung by means of chains in the porch. Inside, however, the long, low church is instantly pleasing, partly because of the soft colouring of its east window (1899). In the sanctuary is the stone effigy of a knight holding a heart in his hand. One of the brasses under the carpet near the communion rails is to Isobel Fleming who died in 1639:

> Reader here before thine eyes
> A widdow and a wonder lyes,
> Her oyle she spent and yet had store
> By scattering she gathered more . . .

In the churchyard is an old cross with a sort of peephole in the top. Cross Fell (2,930 feet) towers near the village. It was in olden times known as Fiends' Fell and was said to be the haunt of evil spirits until St. Paulinus erected a cross and an altar on its summit. Not far from the road are three artificial terraces known, for no discoverable reason, as the Hanging Walls of Mark Anthony. They are not really worth the trouble of a visit.

Nearby Blencarn, the 'hill with a cairn', has the post office, Wesleyan chapel of 1840, and a school.

Still along the foothills of the Pennines is Milburn, 'mill stream', the most northerly village in Westmorland. Experts believe that Milburn has retained to an unusual degree its original twelfth-century form. In those days there was always danger of Scottish raids, and all the houses were built facing inwards round a rectangular village green. The only entrances were a narrow one at each corner. These could be walled up every winter, and this was in fact continued until 1826. Narrow, easily-defended gaps between the houses, called 'through-gangs', were then the only means of entry into the village. One or two of these can still be seen. The cattle could, for safety, be driven on to the large green within the houses. On the village green is a maypole set in the base of an ancient cross. Dancing round it is no longer carried on, and it sports a weathervane, made in the village and put up when the new maypole was installed in 1953 for the Coronation of Elizabeth II. The bus shelter, built by a village craftsman, was erected at the same time, and the chestnut tree in front of the school was then planted. The school is at the far end of the village green and was established before 1790. The post office and general stores are in a bleak, barn-like building. The parish hall, 1912, and church lie outside the village, to the south-west. The church, of St. Cuthbert, is a simple one set in the midst of fields. It is mostly Norman and very plain. The interior was completely renovated in 1894. There is no pub, but some half mile away is 'The Stag Inn', opposite a road leading to Howgill Castle, now a farm. At one time the castle belonged to Colonel Honeywood, who was wounded in the Clifton skirmish with Bonnie Prince Charlie's men. He recovered, and was later M.P. for Appleby for many years.

Dufton, 'dove farm', is a very pleasant village, largely of red sandstone, astride a winding country lane. It was formerly a popular haunt for visitors, in particular those in search of geological specimens and the ferns which grow in Dufton Gill and Maize Beck Scar, or for those seeking the pure air of the almost Alpine surroundings. A footpath from the village leads to the Pennine Way via Great Dun Fell, 2,780 feet. Dufton is the centre of the Helm Wind country. The oblong village green is planted with trees and has a fountain given by an official of the London Lead Company. The whitewashed school, no longer in use, is at one end of the green, with a Conservative and Unionist Club (1911) nearby. There is a Primitive Methodist church, 1905, but the old Wesleyan chapel is now a private house with a broken-nosed stone figure of Wesley in a niche half way up the wall. The post office-store is opposite the fountain. The pub is another 'Stag Inn'. There is a house dated 1729. The isolated church of St. Cuthbert lies between Dufton and Knock, across a field. It is a plain church with a gallery, and existed as early as 1293 but was rebuilt in 1784 and thoroughly restored in 1853. Some of the bodies in its churchyard were transported on horseback from a distance of eight miles away.

Narrow, winding lanes through typical Pennine limestone country with its lichen-covered dry-stone walls lead to Murton.

What there is of the village lies at right angles to the road with Murton Fell (2,207 feet) above. The unattractive church, dedicated to St. John the Baptist, is beside the road between Murton and Hilton. Its only real interest lies in its three-decker pulpit facing south. The church and the pulpit are modern, 1856. The oil lamps by which it used to be lighted still stand at the ends of the pews. The burial ground was laid out in 1901. Hilton is slightly larger than Murton and has a store and a pub, 'The Cross Keys'. It has much the appearance of a Yorkshire dales village. It is very quiet, standing off the Appleby road, and is right on the edge of the Ministry of Defence weapon testing area. Christopher Bainbridge born at Hilton in 1464, became Archbishop of York in 1508. Henry VIII sent him as ambassador to the Pope the following year. He became a cardinal in 1511 and was given command of the Pope's army against France. He was poisoned, reputedly by his own steward, an Italian priest, and died in 1514. He is buried in the English College in Rome.

Lovely tree-lined roads lead to the village of Long Marton. Apart from one or two exceptions it is a very pleasing mixture of old and new houses. One of the oldest is a cottage built for 'John Bellas and Margaret his wife 1740'. This is close to 'The Masons Arms'. There is a post office-store, and a Methodist chapel dated 1818 up a long flight of steps. The rather ugly parish institute was built in 1893. The school, near the church, was erected by subscription in 1833. Between the village and its church is the Trout Beck over which a five-arched viaduct carries the Settle–Carlisle railway. The village station is no longer used. The eleventh to twelfth-century church is dedicated to St. Margaret and St. James, and was thoroughly restored in 1880. Most interesting to me are the strange carvings over the doorways. Pevsner calls the one over the south doorway a 'forceful and barbaric tympanum'. This, and the one over the west doorway, is of Norman or earlier work, and its dragon theme is doubtless linked with the legend which tells of a dragon appearing in St. Margaret's prison cell and swallowing her. It is a lovely church with delightful stonework in its windows. The chancel roof is beautifully carved and has an electric light switch so that it can be illuminated for inspection. The Royal Arms are those of George II, 1750, and are quite crudely painted.

There is an Elizabethan table which belonged to the church, was lost, and was found by the present rector in a barn. One of several interesting tombstones in the churchyard is that of William Bellasis, 'an officer of the ship Scaleby Castle' who died at sea on a voyage to the East Indies aged twenty-three.

Crackenthorpe is now a quiet village, although still within earshot of the steady hum of traffic along the A66 to the south. Crackenthorpe Hall to the south, near the Eden, was for long the home of the Machell family, one of whom, Roger, was drowned at Cyprus while crusading with Richard Coeur de Lion. Roger Head to the east is named after him. After the Battle of Hexham (1464) Henry VI wandered about the hills of Yorkshire and Westmorland for some months and at Crackenthorpe Hall he found shelter on more than one occasion. He is supposed to have disguised himself as a gardener there, once when his pursuers were close.

Although it is the site of the Roman camp of Bravoniacum I found Kirkby Thore a rather uninteresting village with little character. Gypsum is mined nearby for the manufacture of plaster board and the many new houses must have come into being to house the workers. There is a stone cottage dated 1751. The village lies mainly to the north of the A66 but the pub is beside the main road. It is 'The Bridge End Inn', doubtless named after the bridge over the Trout Beck. The Wesleyan chapel of 1828 continues as a Methodist church, and there is a war memorial hall (1914–18) the foundation stone of which was laid by Lord Hothfield in 1926. The school is on the outskirts of the village, and the church, too, stands rather away from the present village. It is dedicated to St. Michael and a considerable portion of its structure is Norman. The carved pulpit is dated 1631. The church bell, cast at York in 1450, is probably the largest in Westmorland. The font cover was given in memory of Thomas Machell, the antiquary, who was rector at Kirkby Thore from 1677 to 1698. A crucifix hangs from the chancel arch. There is a memorial tablet to the fallen in both world wars by the font, and a number of coats of arms on the walls. These include the families of Machell, Warcop and Wharton. General Bowser, K.G.C.B., who became Commander-in-Chief of the Madras Army, was born at Kirkby Thore in 1748.

There are at least ten places called Newbiggin, or 'new building', in the area covered by this book. The one now mentioned is only a small cluster of houses, almost on the Cumberland border. Its church is dedicated to St. Edmund and was built in 1853–4 on the site of the former church. It has an old sundial on a buttress near the entrance and a more recent one just inside the churchyard gate. There is an interesting panel giving the 121st Psalm above the door. The ceiling is decorated with stars. Newbiggin Hall, next to the church, was rebuilt by Christopher Crackenthorpe in 1533. An unusual bell-tower stands between it and the church. It is used, the present owner told me, for calling people in to meals. A Wesleyan chapel of 1880 stands in the village neglected and empty.

Lying like Kirkby Thore just to the north of the A66 is Temple Sowerby, often referred to as the 'Queen of Westmorland villages'. It seems appropriate, therefore, that its pub should be 'The King's Arms'. The village gets its name, of course, from the Knights Templars who once owned Sowerby Manor, which was transferred in 1323 by Act of Parliament, soon after the suppression of their order, to the Knights Hospitallers. Now known as Acorn Bank it was bequeathed to the National Trust by Dorothy Una Ratcliffe, the authoress, in 1950. There is an old mill with two water wheels in its grounds. The post office and store is nearby. Most of the pleasant, spacious village lies around its village green. A house near the church is dated 1616. The church is dedicated to St. James and was a very small one until 1770 when it was rebuilt on a much larger scale. In 1875 extensive repairs and restoration were undertaken and the nave and chancel were largely rebuilt. The first clock was installed in the tower in 1807 and this was replaced in 1951 by an electrically wound one. A mark near the church porch proclaims it to be 348¾ feet above the sea. The village hall is the Victory Memorial Hall, 1914–18. There is a school with a single bell-cote and bell and close to it the Methodist church dated 1872, unusually standing back in a small pleasant garden. Beside its porch is a stone from which John Wesley preached in 1782. A little over half a mile east of the village is a Roman milestone, standing four foot six inches high on the grass verge at a lay-by beside the main A66 road.

4

The South-east—from Penrith to Burton-in-Kendal

THIS chapter can be divided into two parts—its northern sector with a large group of villages south of the A66 and down into the wild Mallerstang area; and the southern sector, south of the wasp waist where the Yorkshire boundary squeezes westwards almost to the M6 motorway. Like the north-eastern chapter, it embraces some of the loveliest moorland scenery one can find anywhere.

Most people are too busy dashing through the interesting village of Eamont Bridge to notice it very much. It lies astride the old A6 trunk road and it must have seen, over the centuries, a succession of many thousands of travellers hastening northwards or southwards. The name stands for 'junction of streams' and the village is also the boundary between Cumberland and Westmorland. Most of the houses and cottages look old. On the Cumberland side of the river are two dated 1734 and 1784. The first house into Westmorland is dated 1671 and carries the Latin inscription '*Omne solum forti patria est*'—the cry of the exile from Ovid 'Every soil is a fatherland to a brave man'. Opposite the disused village hall is a large house dated 1686, and another nearby was built in 1719. The tiny post office is dated 1744. There are two pubs opposite each other, the earlier, 'The Crown Hotel', is dated 1720. 'The Beehive Inn', 1727, was once kept by a Jacobite chaplain, who turned innkeeper after the failure of the 1745 Rebellion. It has carried the following rhyme above its door for very many years:

Within this hive we are all alive,
Good liquor makes us funny;
If you be dry, step in and try
The flavour of our honey.

What looks like a more recent war memorial, near 'The Crown Hotel', is actually, and unusually, a tribute to the four volunteers from the village who went to the South African War. In the field behind it is Arthur's Round Table, a circular Henge monument used for religious purposes and dating from about 1800 B.C. The Scottish army accompanying Charles II to Worcester camped within it. A little way down the Yanwath road, and at the side of the motorway, is another Henge monument, Mayborough, dating from about 2,000 B.C. On the Brougham road is a church full of remarkable medieval woodwork and possessing a truly magnificent Flemish altar-piece, removed at present for restoration and then exhibition at the Victoria and Albert Museum, South Kensington, until about 1976. It is costing about £5,000 to restore. The church is Brougham chapel, built in the fourteenth century and well worth a visit.

Clifton, a short distance away along the A6, is within earshot of the motorway, which runs parallel in a cutting. What is left of Clifton Hall can be seen clearly from the motorway. The name Clifton means 'the place on a hill'. The part-Norman church is dedicated to St. Cuthbert. It has a cool, plain interior with little stained class. The most interesting window is a portrait of Eleanor Engayne, who was married in 1365; there is also a memorial tablet to her in the north wall. Another window commemorates a Captain of the East India Company's artillery service who died at Mysore. These windows in the east end were the only two saved when an explosion of gas in 1942 blew out all the windows and brought down the ceiling. There are carvings of the Adoration on the pulpit. The roll of honour to the men of the 1914–18 war is in the church. In the churchyard, just inside the gate, a stone pays tribute to the 'memory of the Troopers of Bland's Regiment who lie here killed at Clifton Moor 1745'. This skirmish is described by Scott in *Waverley*. It took place when the advance party of the Duke of Cumberland's army caught up with the rearguard of Bonnie Prince Charlie's men. At the opposite end of the village is a farm, Town End, owned at the time by a Quaker, Thomas Savage. Savage managed to signal the positions of the Highlanders to Cumberland's men, and the Duke lodged that night at the farm with Savage. Behind some barns only a stone's-throw from the road still stands the oak tree under which the Highlanders were buried, and a plate marks the spot.

The village hall is almost opposite the church. The post office-store is next to the Wesleyan chapel, 1885. The Lowther Park Caravan Site, opened in 1971, can be seen from the village across the motorway; it must be one of the finest caravan sites in England. The 'Clifton Hill Hotel' is also a motel. The humbler, more hospitable, 'George and Dragon' is close to Town End farm. Wetheriggs Pottery was started in Clifton in 1855. It is probably best known for its hen-and-chicken money-boxes, although it originally made only roof tiles and bricks.

Listed as a 'village' Melkinthorpe is no more than a row of not very interesting or distinguished buildings forming a cul-de-sac mid-way between Clifton and Cliburn, a pleasant, quiet village mostly on the Morland road. The school is on the road to Temple Sowerby, the pub is 'The Golden Pheasant', and there is a Wesleyan chapel dated 1852. Cliburn means 'cliff stream', and it is from the church of St. Cuthbert that one can see why it was so called. There are wonderful views all around. The church is largely Norman but was thoroughly restored in 1887. It possesses a chest dated 1690. Its font cover is in memory of Admiral Christopher J. Cleborne (1839–1909), M.D., of the U.S. Navy, a descendant of the Cliburns of Cliburn Hall, and there is a window in memory of his third son. The pride of the church is one of the most perfect and best preserved early Jerusalem crosses in existence. It came from Vallambrossa monastery in Italy where it had been for about seven hundred years until the monastery's suppression by King Victor Emmanuel. Made from Gethsemane olive inlaid with ebony and pearl, it was given to the church by Admiral Cleborne. The Elizabethan hall, now a farmhouse, is across the road from the church.

Bolton is a picturesque and spaciously laid-out village aptly named a 'place of dwellings', for new houses are spreading along its roads and enlarging it greatly. It has a memorial hall built in

1922 to commemorate the 1914–18 war, and a post office-general store. The pub is 'The New Crown'. At the church of All Saints one is greeted at the porch by a tombstone bearing a skull-and-crossbones, and nearby, let into the church wall, is the stone effigy of a praying figure, probably a lady. It is yet another mostly-Norman church, with its twelfth-century doorway patterned with six-petalled rosettes and figured capitals. Above another Norman doorway, now a window, on the north side, is a slab bearing a carving of two knights jousting. Just inside the church on the right is 'The Pour man's box' dated 1634. The font cover, on the left, is dated 1687. The font looks ancient but bears no date. Above the door is an interesting 'Benefactors' board. The Royal Arms are those of Queen Victoria. The chancel arch has a lovely carved screen. There is a Methodist chapel in the village built in 1818 and restored in 1926.

Another place listed as a village but much more of a hamlet today is Colby—'the coal (or charcoal) place'. There is a United Methodist Free Church built in 1874; a corrugated iron church, unused and in a sorry state; some riding stables; and little else.

Despite its rather high-sounding name King's Meaburn is little more than a long line of houses on each side of the road. The pub is 'The White Horse Inn'. There is a village hall, 1919, and nearby a house dated 1827 and another 1789. The school was 'erected and endowed by subscription' in 1831. It has a post office and 'The Shop', and a Methodist church dated 1932. The royal ring to the village's name comes from a tragic incident in the country's history. The early manor of Meaburn included this and Mauld's Meaburn, to the south, held by Roger de Morville. At his death he divided it between his son and his daughter, Hugh and Maud. Hugh was implicated in the murder of Thomas à Becket (1170) and for this the King seized his portion of the manor and since then the two Meaburns have been known as King's Meaburn and Maud's (or Mauld's) Meaburn. Lancelot Addison, the father of the famous essayist Joseph Addison, was born at Mauld's Meaburn in 1632.

Morland, the 'grove by a moor', is a quiet hilly village with lovely views up the Eden valley. It has a school, originally established some time before 1779, a village hall, a post office, and a village craft shop. At one time a market and a fair were held (now long obsolete), and early in the last century linen manufacture was carried on in two factories. There are two pubs, 'The Crown Inn' and 'The King's Arms'. The latter is dated 1807 and there is a house dated 1814 beside it. The church, dedicated to St. Lawrence, is solid and ancient-looking. According to Pevsner it has the only Anglo-Saxon west tower in Cumberland and Westmorland. It is a fascinating church even though it was thoroughly restored in 1896. The Royal Arms are those of George III. It has a 'Poor man's box 1648' and the font is dated 1662 with a cover that looks older. There is not a great deal of stained glass but the east window is beautiful. It, and the carved oak reredos, are 1926. An unusual brass is mounted so that both sides can be seen. On one side it is a memorial to John Blyth, vicar, who died in 1562. The other side depicts a sixteenth-century knight. The pulpit is dated 1721 and its canopy 1722. The communion rails are Jacobean, and some lovely faces have been carved, by a cunning hand, on an old beam in front of the organ. There is an interesting inscription to John Thompson, schoolmaster, who died in 1736. The war memorial in the churchyard includes the Boer War. Memorial tablets for the two world wars are inside the church.

Newby, the 'new settlement', is a pleasant, small village south-west of Morland. It has a house dated 1692 but little else to commend it.

Another village without very much of interest is Great Strickland. It was listed in Domesday Book as 'Stircaland'—'pasture for young bullocks'. It possesses a village hall, a house dated 1746, a Wesleyan Methodist chapel of 1887, and the 'Lowther Castle Hotel'. Ecclesiastically it forms part of the parish of Thrimby, with Little Strickland. Its unprepossessing church of St. Barnabas was built in 1870 as a chapel-of-ease to the mother church at Little Strickland. Its east end forms an apse with the only three stained glass windows. An unnecessarily elaborate and rather ugly crucifix stands on the altar. Little Strickland, to the south, contains the small simple church of St. Mary, Thrimby, built in 1814. It has no ornamentation and no stained glass. A seventeenth-century carved stone is set into the porch wall. Next to the church is the village school. Both buildings have a single bell-cote, but only that of the church contains a bell. There is a corrugated-iron village hall. One house is dated 1719; another dated 1826 looks as though it might have been the pub, 'The Greyhound'. The Hall, now a farm, is on the hill above the village green.

In this small area I found the villages of little merit; another is Sleagill—the 'trickling, or slavering, stream'. It has houses dated 1760 and 1823 and a comparatively recent Methodist church built in 1954. Two rather forlorn swings were obviously the village's contribution to the present Queen's coronation, and bear the legend 'E II R 1953'. Hoff, too, is hardly worthy of the name 'village'. It is a small cluster of houses on the B6260 Appleby–Orton road. Near its pub, 'The New Inn', was the 1895 Methodist chapel—now empty and being converted into a private house. The name stands for a 'house' or 'temple'. Near Hoff Bridge, in the days of Richard II, a battle was fought between the English and the Scots, and spears and swords have been found during ploughing.

Of considerable interest is Great Ormside, in a cul-de-sac not far south of the A66. The village is gathered round a triangular village green. One farm is dated 1683, another 1687. The village was 'the seat of Orm the Viking' and Viking weapons found there in 1899 are now in Carlisle Museum. The grey stone church stands on a hill beside the river Eden and beyond the village. Close to it is the ten-arched viaduct of the Settle–Carlisle Railway, built over the Eden in 1870–5. The church is dedicated to St. James and the way to it is through the yard of a farm which was formerly Ormside Hall. In the churchyard is an ancient cross socket dated 1643 but the shaft in it is no earlier than 1897. The church is a scheduled historical monument and has been a place of burial and worship for about two thousand years. It has neither spire nor tower, but a short square base to a gabled roof. The porch and walls contain various old stones and a mutilated Roman altar. The oak roof is seventeenth-century. There is no stained glass, but there is a fascinating leper squint near the altar rail. The north aisle has the Hilton chapel which was used for years as the village school. The Hilton arms in it are dated 1723 but the chapel is earlier. The roll of honour and memorial tablet to those who fell in the 1914–18 war are in the church. The ninth-century gold and silver Ormside Cup was found in the churchyard in 1823. It is now in York Museum. The will of the Black Prince is said to have been drawn up by John, priest of Ormside.

A very attractive village set in a wooded hollow is Great Asby, the 'settlement where the ash trees grew'. Both the village and its green lie on both banks of a stream which also separates the rector from his church. Two footbridges and a road bridge connect the two sides of the village. At one end of the village green is a seat given by the Women's Institute. Behind it is St. Helen's Almshouse built between 1811 and 1818. Beside the stream is the famous St. Helen's Well reputed never to run dry or freeze. Across the nearby footbridge is Asby Hall with the Musgrave arms and initials above its door, and the date 1694. The pub is directly opposite the church. It is 'The Three Greyhounds' and has the post office-general stores next door. There is a village hall dated 1859 and a Baptist chapel built in 1862. The church was consecrated in 1866 on the site of an older one. It is dedicated to St. Peter and episodes from his life are shown in the glass of the east window. Modern glass in the south aisle depicts St. Peter and St. Bartholomew. Carvings of musicians support the roof beams. The church has a twin bell-cote, and the churchyard is entered under a lych gate. Thomas Smith (1615–1702) was born at Whitewall just outside the village; he became Bishop of Carlisle in 1684.

Another very pleasant village is Crosby Ravensworth. It is on the pretty Lyvennet which runs beside the main road; across it lies the church. It is a village with plenty of trees and much character. The church, dedicated to St. Lawrence, has existed since the twelfth century and probably earlier, though it has suffered alterations and restorations, some because of the Scottish wars. The doorway is Early English and the octagonal font is dated 1662. In 1811, it is said, a sycamore tree grew out of the tower and the walls were leaning and dangerous. It was restored then, in part by Robert Smirke who was working at the time at Lowther Castle, and then restored yet again between 1865 and 1880. The carved reredos was added in 1897. Largely responsible for the 1811 restoration was George Gibson, and there is a memorial to him in the west end of the church. The memorial, with figures representing Faith, Hope and Charity, was the work of David Dunbar (1792–1866), a Dumfries-born sculptor who had studios in both Carlisle and Newcastle, and whose work is in both those cathedrals. He was the first artist on the spot after Grace Darling performed her heroic feat,[1] and the Bishop of Durham bought Dunbar's bust of her. The village has two pubs, 'The Sun Hotel' and 'The Butchers Arms', the latter dated 1853. The 1927 village hall has a well-kept air and carries plaques to those who served in both world wars. The post office is a private house. There is a Wesleyan Methodist chapel dated 1875.

The road from either Great Asby or Crosby Ravensworth to Orton is through some of the loveliest scenery in Westmorland. Orton is a large thriving village and the centre of a small network of roads. It has a post office-store, and another store, and two pubs—'The Waverley Temperance Hotel' and 'The George Hotel'. It also possesses a temperance hall dated 1858. Near 'The George Hotel' is a house carrying the date 1604. Orton Hall on the opposite side of the road was built in 1662 and was the home of Richard Burn, vicar of Orton from 1736 until his death in 1785. He is best known for his collaboration with Joseph Nicolson in producing the first history of Westmorland and Cumberland in 1777, and for his legal writings. The Wesleyan chapel built in 1833, chiefly at the instigation of Stephen Brunskill, is now the Wesleyan Methodist church. Brunskill was an ardent worker and writer for Wesleyanism. George Whitehead (1636–1723), one of the chief founders of the Society of Friends, was born at Orton. The present school is very modern, but the first school was built in 1730 by public subscription. The village has a large number of small footbridges to enable the people to cross from one part to another. The Church of All Saints stands high on a hill. It dates from the thirteenth century. Its octagonal font is dated 1662 and its interesting prayer desk and pulpit are of the same century. So are the Royal Arms, dated 1695, above the door. It is unusual in having roof lights. Three old and large bells are mounted in a frame in the north aisle—one fourteenth-century, the other two

[1] The daughter of a lighthouse-keeper on one of the Farne Islands, Grace Darling (1815–42) heroically risked her life to rescue nine people from a wrecked ship.

The Norman tympanum above the church door at Long Marton

Temple Sowerby church and village

Early sixteenth-century German carved panels at Brougham chapel, near Eamont Bridge

Soulby, on the banks of Scandal Beck

Crosby Garrett, as seen from the churchyard

The church and war memorial at Casterton

The main street at Burton-in-Kendal, with its eighteenth-century market cross dated 1637. Modern stained glass in the south aisle depicts St. Ninian and St. Martin. There is a rather ugly memorial to the fallen in the 1914–18 war, and the gates at the east and west entrances to the churchyard are also memorials.

Warcop, or 'beacon hill', is a large, straggling, spread-out village quite close to the A66. It centres on the lovely sixteenth-century bridge, said to be the only bridge over the Eden to withstand the floods of 1822. Nearby stands the tall maypole on five square steps, originally the base of an ancient cross. It has a pheasant windvane on top. The war memorial to both wars is close by, and there is a memorial tablet in the church. There is a post office-store, and another store. The pub is 'The Chamley Arms', formerly 'The Railway Inn'. Opposite is the only remaining smithy (of three), surmounted by a lovely weathervane—a man ploughing behind two horses. The reading room was erected in 1877, the Wesleyan chapel in 1872, and the temperance hall in 1865. The school and church stand rather apart from the village to the north-west. The church, dedicated to St. Columba, was sold after the Reformation to the owners of Warcop Hill, and given by the owner to the Bishop of Carlisle as recently as 1957. The churchyard is entered through a lych-gate erected in memory of Captain Henry Preston who was killed in the Crimea. The church has an odd-looking squat turret perched on the west end. It is one where rush-bearing takes place every year; on St. Peter's Day, 29th June, the boys carry crosses made from rushes, and the girls garlands of flowers. There are numbered box-pews. The chancel is surprisingly large. In the sanctuary is a carved chair dated 1684, and there are seats for the officiating clergy. In the south transept is the much-worn stone effigy of a woman. Instruments from the nineteenth-century church band are on display in a glass case.

Despite its proximity to the A66 Great Musgrave—the 'grove frequented by mice'—is very quiet and peaceful with lovely winding lanes round it and good views over open country. There is a house dated 1687 at the eastern end of the village and others look to be a good age; there is very little modern building. The village hall has a neglected air. A post office-store serves the small community. The village is on a hill with its grey towered church, dedicated to St. Theobald, below and beside the river Eden. The present church was built in 1845–6 to take the place of one even closer to the river which, when the Eden was in spate, was flooded pew-deep. A path leads from the village down to the church, or it can be approached by an avenue of fine horse-chestnut trees from the Kirkby Stephen road. This is another church which keeps up the rush-bearing ceremony each year—here on the first Sunday in July. Just inside the communion rail is a brass to Thomas Ouds who died in 1502. It originally had the four evangelists, one at each corner, but now only one remains—the lion of St. Mark. William Paley (1743–1805), famous for his theological writings, was rector from 1775 to 1777. It was over this churchyard wall that the first grayling in the Eden were tipped as fry one night about 1880. The fine, gravelly bed suited the fish and they have multiplied and established themselves.

At a crossroads on the banks of Scandal Beck is Soulby. On the green at one side of the bridge a pump, the 'Royal Jubilee Memorial 1887. Erected by subscription', still stands, surrounded by a low stone wall and very overgrown and neglected. This was for the Queen's Golden Jubilee. Trees nearby were planted for the Diamond Jubilee in 1897. On the opposite bank is the village school (1876). There is a post office-store. The Wesleyan chapel dated 1893 is built on to the earlier, 1833, Methodist chapel which can be seen behind it. The church of St. Luke was built by the Royalist Sir Philip Musgrave after the restoration of Charles II. Sir Philip's arms and the date 1663 are above the porch. It is a pleasant, neat little church, extensively restored in 1874. The font was given in 1877 by Sir R. G. Musgrave. Tablets commemorate the five Soulby men who died in each of the world wars. The church is surmounted by an ornate weathervane dated 1830. A tithe barn, approached by a ramp, is opposite. A nearby house is dated 1682. A Manor Court, held at Soulby as late as 1915, could well be the last to be held in England. Bombs were dropped in a field close to the village by a German aircraft in October 1941. During heavy snows in 1947 the postman and the butcher made their deliveries by sledge.

Crosby Garrett is an isolated village of less than fifty houses with three places of worship. Its most interesting feature is its ancient church of St. Andrew, perched high on a steep hill with panoramic views all round. A church has stood on the hill, looking down on its village, for more than a thousand years; parts of the present one are Anglo-Saxon. It is said that the devil, seeing all the stones ready to build the church at the foot of the hill, carried them to the top in his leather apron, reasoning that as the people grew old they would not be able to climb the hill and would in consequence come his way rather than to heaven! There are interesting carvings on the columns inside the church, particularly on the one beside the font. Apart from its antiquity the church is interesting for the tunnel, or hagioscope, cut through the wall to permit people in the north aisle to see the altar. The roll of honour on the north wall looks older than 1914–18, but is undated. The parish has been united with Soulby since 1953. The old rectory opposite the church gates has a stone dated 1719 above the door but it is certainly much older. It has, in the old part of the house, a stone set in the wall and carved by Edmund Mauleverer in 1637. Mauleverer was ejected from his ministry during the Commonwealth for his loyalty to the King. The two other places of worship are the Baptist church erected in 1815 by George Greenwood, an Independent, and the Wesleyan chapel, 1882. There is a post office-store and a village hall. A cottage by the small bridge joining the two village streets is dated 1691. Just beyond the village can be seen the Smardale Viaduct of the Settle–Carlisle railway. Crosby Garrett station was closed in 1952.

Astride the Brough to Kirkby Stephen road is Brough Sowerby, 'the boggy district near Brough'. It has a house dated 1708 and some quite new building. The pub is 'The Black Bull'. A new Methodist chapel was opened in 1972 to replace the former corrugated iron building which had been built in 1897. Before that, services had been held in the homes of members.

Kaber, 'jackdaw hill', is no more than a few houses and farms with a huge village green, and a surprisingly large Methodist chapel rebuilt in 1891. One house is dated 1732 and another 1774. The school was 'rebuilt by the landowners in the township of Kaber 1862' and another plaque on it records that Anthony Morland left money from which a field was purchased 'the yearly income from which is to be paid to the master yearly for ever'. An even more interesting inscription was above the door of the old school. It read:

A yeoman of this town did live
Till he was old and then did give
Unto this school the yearly sum
Of eight pounds for each year to come.
That children may be taught therein
Behaviour and good discipline;
His name, and age, and day of death
May all be seen here underneath.

Thomas Waller, the donor, he died October the 17th, 1689.
In the 79th year of his age.

South of Kirkby Stephen is Nateby, a small village at the beginning of some lovely wild scenery with the road to Swaledale going one way, and straight on the winding nine-and-a-half-mile scenic road to the Moorcock Inn. To me the village had much kinship with the Yorkshire dales villages. The pub is 'The Black Bull Inn', and there is a village shop, a garage, a Methodist church built in 1875 and, at the south end, the school built in 1877. The river Eden lies to the west.

The Mallerstang Valley is the only part of Cumbria producing its own cheese—very similar to Wensleydale cheese. Along the valley is the village of Outhgill approaching the Yorkshire boundary. It possesses Mallerstang church, dedicated to St. Mary, and probably first built about 1311. It was repaired by Lady Anne Clifford in 1663 and is in present need of restoration. It carries a bell-cote with a most incongruous chimney beside it. The font was made in 1663 and the Royal Arms are dated the same year. The pulpit is 1798. It has a pleasant east window but the rest is rather bleak and bare. There is also a Wesleyan chapel of 1878. The post office-store is nearby, and the village green and hall (not now used) are behind it. The old school, looking rather like a railway station, is perched on the hillside. It is now a Field Centre. The main railway line runs half way up the fell-side west of the village, with Wild Boar Fell (2,324 ft.) pointing to the sky. In the field next to the church is an old water-powered paddle wheel. Just north of the village, and beside the road, is all that remains of Pendragon Castle. Traditionally it was the stronghold of Uther Pendragon, father of King Arthur of the Round Table. It was almost certainly a pele-tower in the twelfth century, burned down by the Scots in 1340, restored, and destroyed once again by the Scots in 1541. Lady Anne Clifford restored it in 1660. It was finally dismantled in 1685.

Along the Kirkby Stephen to Tebay road (A685) is Ravenstonedale, 'the valley with the raven's stone'. It is a clean, well-kept village on both sides of a long, climbing street. It has two pubs, 'The Black Swan Hotel' and 'The King's Head Hotel'. There is a Wesleyan chapel dated 1839, and also a High chapel. A few of the houses look quite old. The school, rebuilt in 1873, was founded in the seventeenth century and a large number of clergymen were educated there. Annual sheep-dog trials are held near the village. The church of St. Oswald was rebuilt in 1744 but is much older. The earlier church had a separate bell tower and rested on pillars. From the centre hung a 'refuge' bell. If anyone guilty of a crime punishable by death escaped to Ravenstonedale, and managed to toll the bell, he was free from arrest by the King's officers. The privilege was abolished in the reign of James I. The churchyard is full of lovely yew trees. It has a sundial dated 1700, and a curious tombstone which reads:

> 1786. Here lies a wife Mary Metcalf.
> Where I was born, or when, it matters not
> To whom related, or by whom begot.

Inside the church are several unusual features. The box pews are arranged so that the two halves of the congregation face each other, north and south. There are few churches in the country so arranged. The three-decker pulpit is from the old church. It has a sounding board and, another scarce thing, a seat for the parson's wife behind the top tier. The Royal Arms are of George II. A 1610 hourglass, a tuning fork for the choir, and a pitch pipe for starting hymns are on display in a case under the gallery. A painted wooden clock-face dated 1719 is preserved from the old church. One window in the east end is particularly interesting as it commemorates the last woman to suffer death in England in the cause of the Protestant faith. She was Elizabeth Gaunt, sentenced by the notorious Judge Jefferies to be burnt at Tyburn in 1685. William Penn was one of the crowd who attended her execution.

Not far from Ravenstonedale is Newbiggin-on-Lune. It is a small, compact village. Its tiny church of St. Aidan was built in 1892 and has on the outside a plaque to the only man from the village who was killed in the 1914–18 war. There is a Methodist church opened in 1939; a national school dated 1872 and a public hall of 1925. Post office, store, garage and houses make up the rest of the village.

Tebay lies just east of the motorway and can be seen clearly from it. The older part of the village consists of stone cottages, while the more modern part was centred around the railway. The church was in fact erected in 1880 for the railwaymen who lived and worked on the lines. It is dedicated to St. James and faced with Shap granite. The interior is brick-lined in yellow with red bands. The west end is a large apse. A memorial window on the north side is to the fallen in the 1914–18 war and a tablet on the wall beneath is to the 1939–45 war. The village itself is long and uninteresting. Quite a lot of the building is of flat Westmorland slates. There are two pubs, 'The Cross Keys Inn' and 'The Junction Hotel'. A Primitive Methodist chapel is dated 1885 and there is a post office and several other shops.

Three villages on or close to the quite busy A683 are Casterton, Barbon and Middleton. Casterton, 'the place by a Roman fort', is an attractive village, mostly of grey stone, nestling in the hills above the lovely river Lune. Charlotte Brontë received a short part of her education, from 1824–5, at a School for Clergymen's Daughters founded in 1823 at Cowan Bridge just over the Yorkshire border. The school moved to Casterton in 1833 and became Casterton School. She refers to it in *Jane Eyre*. Brontë House, formerly The Servants' School, lies west of the road, on the opposite side to the unattractive church. Dedicated to the Holy Trinity, the church was built in 1831–3 and paid for by the Rev. Carus Wilson, to be a chapel for the School as well as the parish church. Inside it is of a bleak, barn-like structure, yet Queen Adelaide is reported to have thought it beautiful. When I was there some girls from the School were ringing the bells, and their high-pitched chatter inside the church together with the noise of the bells outside was far from peaceful. I was impressed most by two rather fine single windows in the west end based on the Benedicite. They were designed in 1897–9 by Henry Holiday (1839–1927), as were both the windows and the paintings in the chancel. Paintings of biblical scenes, on canvas, are stuck to the walls all round the church. Those not painted by Henry Holiday are by James Clarke. Holiday was a friend of Burne-Jones and Holman Hunt, and Hunt's influence is evident. There is a rather unusual carved wooden reredos above the altar. The small window to R. A. Burton in the west end was broken by burglars in 1910. The war memorial to those who fell in both World Wars stands beside the main road near the church. The pub is the Casterton Hotel. Wild strawberries grow plentifully along the sides of the village lanes.

A hotch-potch of houses and cottages, many of them whitewashed, lies east of the A683 where Barbon Beck tumbles off the fells to meet the Lune. Barbon, 'the stream of the bear', was formerly a railway halt, but the station is derelict and the lines no longer there. The unpretentious but lovely church near the station was built in 1893 and is dedicated to St. Bartholomew; a carving of him is over the porch entrance. In its sanctuary is a carved chair dated 1662. But perhaps most noteworthy is the east window; this is in clear glass, perhaps left deliberately so as through it can be seen Crag Hill, 2,239 ft. With how much more meaning can the choir and congregation join in the 121st Psalm —'I will lift up mine eyes unto the hills. . . .' The oak lych-gate through which the churchyard is entered was put there in 1915. There is a village hall (1926), a post office with the war memorial close by, and between it and the church the deservedly well-known 'Barbon Inn'. Opposite the Wesleyan chapel (1888) is a road leading down to an old pack-horse bridge.

Middleton church, dedicated to the Holy Ghost, lies beside the A683. It was rebuilt in 1878–9 on the site of an earlier church. It has little of interest except perhaps a window to commemorate the Diamond Jubilee of Queen Victoria. 'The Swan Inn' is not far away but, although the place is listed as a village, there is no coherent cluster of houses. Middleton Hall, east of the road, is accessible to the public, the medieval curtain-wall being a scheduled ancient monument.

West of the Lune and reached by hilly, narrow, winding lanes is Killington, 'the place of Cylla's people'. When I last visited it the high banks which hem you in on both sides of the narrow lanes were illuminated by masses of bluebells. The church is almost all there is to see, but it is by itself worth the visit. It is an ancient one, dedicated to All Saints and restored in 1895. Hanging above the centre aisle are the oil lamps which once lighted it, and on each side of the pulpit is a candle in a brass holder. (The church is, however, now lighted by electricity.) Recessed windows show its thick walls. The bell-rope is reached by climbing an open wooden stair inside the church. The original chapel was built by the Pickering family for the convenience of the residents of the Hall and their tenants. After the Reformation it was, perforce, disused, and the practising of religion was almost impossible. In 1585 the inhabitants petitioned the Bishop of Chester, to whose diocese they then belonged, to have divine service in the chapel because—'by reason of . . . the storms and inundations which often raged in their hilly district in the winter season, they could not carry their dead to be buried without great trouble and inconvenience, nor their children to be baptised without great peril both of soul and body, nor resort thither to hear Divine service and receive the Sacraments as beseemeth good Christians, and by right they are bounden'. The Bishop granted them his licence. Killington Hall, opposite the church, is now partly in ruins and partly a farm house. There is a village hall, little used, but no post office, shop, pub nor bus service. The former 'Red Lion' pub is now a private house. Even here, week-end cottages bought by people from Liverpool are beginning to upset the balance of village life.

The only other place between the river Lune and the motorway north of the A65 is Mansergh. It is perhaps more of a parish than a village, for the church is Mansergh church, dedicated to St. Peter, and about half-a-mile distant along a narrow lane from the village of Old Town. The church, with its weathercock slightly awry, is magnificently sited, looking over miles and miles of lovely, rolling, wooded countryside. It was built, according to a tablet on its west end, in 1880 on the site of the original church of 1726. Beneath the tablet is the war memorial. The Roll of Honour is inside the church. It is a plain, simple church with a plastered wagon roof and mostly clear glass windows. Its font is of white marble imported from New Zealand. Where the lane starts to lead up to the church is Rigmaden school, built in 1839. Old Town lies on the Kirkby Lonsdale to Kendal road and is nothing more than a few houses—no pub or other amenities. One large house has the date 1608, rebuilt 1847, above its door, while over one window are the initials EC with the dates 1542–1910. The Conder family lived here for almost 370 years and EC will be Edward Conder who was buried at Kirkby Lonsdale in 1542.

The stone from which Mansergh church is built came from quarries south of the A65 at Hutton Roof. This grey forgotten village which has been described as 'romantic' is dominated to the west by barren crags of outcroppings of grey limestone. Some of the village buildings are sadly in need of repair. There is a post office-store, but no pub. The former Wesleyan chapel built in 1850 still carries above its date a scroll, bearing the words 'God is love', carved so as to stand out in relief almost like theatre curtains in miniature. The chapel was used as the headquarters of the local Home Guard during the 1939–45 war; it is now a private garage. There is a rather dilapidated-looking village hall. About a quarter of a mile outside the village on the Lupton road is the church of St. John built in 1881–2 to replace a chapel of 1757. In the farthest corner of the churchyard near the road is the war memorial in the form of a rough craggy stone. It carries the names of four men of Hutton Roof who gave their lives in the 1914–18 war. One, Theodore B. Hardy, was the schoolmaster and vicar. He was awarded the V.C., the D.S.O., and the M.C. for saving and helping the wounded as an army chaplain, and was killed shortly before hostilities ceased. A short distance along the road from the church towards Lupton is a house, Badger Gate, which was built in 1781.

There is little of Lupton on the main A65 road. A few houses and farms and a pub, 'The Plough', are all that can be seen. The church, dedicated to All Saints and built in 1868, is up a lane, signposted 'Old Town', quite a distance to the east of the pub. It is a plain church with an apse at the east end with three windows. There is a cross suspended under the chancel arch. The font is said to be from Kirkby Lonsdale church. The school stands next to the church. Lupton is listed in the Domesday Book as Lupetun and has passed through the hands of the Redman, Harrington, Bellingham and Hutton families. It was purchased by Sir Christopher Musgrave of Eden Hall (see Chapter 3) in 1681 and later belonged to the Earl of Lonsdale.

Nearby Farleton is no more than a handful of grey houses and buildings, lying at the foot of towering Farleton Fell which looks higher than its 801 feet. The village is along a narrow winding lane to the east of the A6070. At the beginning of the present century it had its Prize Ploughing, Horse Show, and Hedging and Walling Association. The old Lancaster Canal lies close by with the new motorway only a stone's throw distant.

The southernmost village, which completes these chapters about the villages to the east of the motorway, is Burton-in-Kendal. From its churchyard the motorway can be seen only a few hundred yards away. It is an ancient village, recorded in Domesday Book as Bortun. Sir James Harrington was granted lands at Burton for his services in capturing poor King Henry VI, at the end of his wanderings in the north after the defeat at Hexham. A market was established at Burton in 1661 and by the middle of the following century it was the most extensive corn market in the country. Decline, however, came shortly after the opening of the Lancaster to Kendal canal in 1819. The market has been obsolete for many years. The village today is large, with a great deal of new building, but along its long Main Street it still retains an air of old world distinction. Its two inns, 'The King's Arms' and 'The Royal Hotel', indicate its earlier importance as one of the chief changing places for horses in the days of pack-horses and stage-coaches, for Burton is about half-way between Lancaster and Kendal. The first stage-coach passed through in 1763. In the market place stands the eighteenth-century market cross, and four recesses can be seen in its steps for leg-irons. Presumably the miscreant sat on the cross steps with his ankles shackled to the riser. There are some strange-sounding street names—Boon Walk, Neddy Hill, Cocking Yard, Tanpits Lane and Jones's Yard are a few. The church, dedicated to St. James, is largely Norman but was thoroughly restored in 1844 and again in 1872. It is a large spacious church with an air of strength and comfort. Its pulpit is Jacobean, about 1607, and there is a chair dated 1782 in the sanctuary. A brass panel attached to the organ commemorates those who fell in the 1939–45 war, and a panel in the church and the war memorial in the churchyard are both to the fallen in the 1914–19 war—presumably it went on for a year longer at Burton! Opposite the church gate is an old house dated 1689. Behind the house is the old school erected in 1817 and restored in 1887, still bearing over its door the inscription 'In commemoration of the Jubilee, June 21st 1887, of our gracious Queen Victoria, this school was restored and enlarged by the inhabitants of Burton and Dalton'. Burton Memorial Hall, 1956, is large, modern and prosperous looking—much more a community centre than a village hall.

5

Along the Coast—from Carlisle to Maryport

THE villages between the Solway Firth and the A595 and A596 are all on the coastal plain. Only two lie north of the river Eden; and the north Solway coast is in Scotland.

Although it is only four and three quarter miles from the city of Carlisle, the delightful village of Rockcliffe has an air of placid remoteness. New development has reached it in the last few years but it retains its genuine village feel and is little spoilt. It stands right on the north bank of the Eden and at the appropriate times of year it is a common sight to see (and often hear) skeins of geese making their way in formation south from the Arctic and later returning north again. The marshes west of Rockcliffe are a famous stopping place for migrant birds. The main Scottish army with Bonnie Prince Charlie crossed the Eden slightly west of the village on 9th November 1745, on their way to attack Carlisle. The red cliffs which gave the place its name stand out beside the water. The pub is 'The Crown and Thistle' (perhaps paying tribute to both sides of the Border?). Opposite is the village hall. There is a post office-general store and, between it and the church, the school built in 1871 and enlarged in 1890. The tall, graceful church spire can be seen for miles around. It was rebuilt to 100 feet in 1881, but on 8th November 1899 it was struck by lightning during a violent thunderstorm and had to be built once again. A later incumbent added the present weathervane of a galleon. He intended this as an indication of Rockcliffe's one-time position as a part of the Port of Carlisle, but ships seem to have a link with the village. A plaque in the north aisle is in memory of Post Captain William Mounsey (1765–1830) of the Royal Navy who, in thirty-five years of service, captured thirty-one enemy ships including the frigate *La Furieuse*, for which last action he received the thanks of the Admiralty and a special gold medal from George III. The church is dedicated to St. Mary, and was rebuilt in 1848. Apart from its stained glass, it is plain and simple; the glass, however, tends to let in only a 'dim, religious light'. The west window, 1881, represents the creation; the east window the crucifixion, resurrection and ascension. In the churchyard, beside the path, is a solid wheel-head cross dating from the tenth or eleventh century. Beside the gate is the memorial to those who died in the two World Wars, with a bronze relief of a steel-helmeted sentry guarding the village. Near the porch is the tombstone of the first incumbent, the Rev. William Robinson who died in 1779 aged eighty-one. It carries a rhyming inscription:

> I, living, planted trees, of one is made
> This chest wherein my body now is laid,
> Which to the grave is brought by God's decree,
> There to remain corruption for to see,
> Till Christ, who is the life, shall come and say—
> Ye dead arise, this is the judgment day.

The allusion is to trees which Robinson planted at a farm where he lodged; there was no vicarage then. He married the farmer's daughter.

Almost half-way between Rockcliffe and Carlisle is Cargo, set back a little from the Eden. It is a mixed and uninteresting village of new bungalows and houses and a few old farms. It is approached past ugly sheds belonging to the Maintenance Unit of the R.A.F. A school was first built in 1854 but this was enlarged and rebuilt in 1897. The former Methodist chapel has been converted into a private house. As with Rockcliffe, a contingent of Jacobite troops passed through Cargo (on 10th November 1745) to cross the Eden to Grinsdale. The name Cargo comes from Carig Howe—'the rocky eminence'. Carlisle Corporation, by virtue of an ancient grant, held certain rights of fishing along the Eden from a spot near Cargo (King Garth) to Etterby. For various reasons this right is no longer exercised, but until eighty or so years ago a complimentary 'fish' dinner was held to the Mayor and Corporation at the house (known as Fish House) which still stands beside the Eden in a field about one mile east of Cargo. It is reached by a lane almost opposite the post office-store. The front of the house is ruined by an amateur-built shelter for boats, but the back has on its walls plaques commemorating the visits of four different mayors, the earliest dated 1751. Another records the visit of 'the first freely elected Mayor of Carlisle' in June 1837. I found lettuces growing in a bath tub in the backyard!

On the south side of the Eden, opposite Cargo and Rockcliffe, are three villages. Nearest to Carlisle is the small farming community of Grinsdale, on both sides of a cul-de-sac off the Burgh road. It consists of little more than a few houses (one dated 1777) and farms, and a church. The tiny, pebble-dashed church on a mound high above the Eden could easily pass unnoticed. It is detached from the village and reached across fields at the village end. It is also hidden behind a clump of trees. The scenery around it is much spoilt by electricity pylons. It is a plain church, and another of the few dedicated to St. Kentigern. The original church was served by a monk from Lanercost until after the dissolution of the monasteries. From then until 1741 no services seem to have been held in it and the building was allowed to become ruinous. It was rebuilt in 1740 and services restarted. The Royal Arms on the west wall are of George III. The building was restored in 1895. The only stained glass, not very good, is in the east window. A memorial slab outside the church includes John Forster 'who died on his passage from Batavia to the Cape of Good Hope' in 1819. On 10th November 1745 a contingent of Bonnie Prince Charlie's army crossed the Eden from Cargo to Grinsdale on their way to capture Carlisle.

There is little noteworthy to see in the lovely tree-lined village of Kirkandrews-upon-Eden. The line of the former Carlisle–Silloth Railway, built in the earlier canal cutting, can be seen plainly. The lines were taken up with almost indecent haste very shortly after the railway closed in 1964, and the station has been converted into a house. A church, 'St. Andrew's Church', may well have stood in the village at one time and given the place its name, but nothing of it remains today except the graveyard along the Beaumont road. It is said that until about 1800 the burial service was read under the shattered remains of the chancel arch which was then standing.

Nearby Beaumont, 'beautiful hill', is a place with a considerable amount of new building. The plain little church of St. Mary was built in the twelfth century on the site of a Roman mile-castle along Hadrian's Wall. Since 1692 it has served as the parish church of both Beaumont and Kirkandrews. It was restored in 1872. Its walled-in east end, with three small windows, looks odd. The font cover is counter-balanced by a lead pigeon which appears, when the lid is on, to be hovering above it. There are two ancient stones let into the west end. The oak beams look to be old. It has memorial tablets to the men who died in both world wars. The bell-cote has a single bell rung from inside the church by means of a chain. The churchyard gates are dated 1897.

Moving now to the beginning of the Solway Firth one comes to Burgh-by-Sands (pronounced 'Bruff'), a large village on a cross roads with many old cottages. Its pub is 'The Greyhound Inn', and there is a post office and two general stores. A public hall was built in 1894. Miniature clogs built by a craftsman in the village were on exhibition on the British stand at the 1972 World Fair at Cologne. On the marshes just outside Burgh King Edward I, 'The Hammer of the Scots', died in 1307. His body lay in state in Burgh church. In 1685 a monument was erected on the spot where local tradition placed his tent. A later monument (1803) still marks the spot. Burgh Marshes are famous locally for their mushrooms. They were also famous in earlier days for their racing, notably for the 'Barony Cup', first given in about 1690. This cup was raced for only when a new Earl of Lonsdale assumed the title. Six of these cups are known; one is referred to in Robert Anderson's ballad 'Burgh Races in 1804':

> The cup was aw siller, and letter'd reet neycely.

The last Barony Cup was competed for in 1883. A National Hunt meeting was inaugurated in April 1882, and confined to hunters until 1892. The last race was in April 1900.

Most notable in Burgh, however, is its church, dedicated to

St. Michael. It was built in 1181, almost entirely with stones from a fort on the Roman Wall. It is one of the few fortified churches—i.e. its tower was built for defence, with narrow windows high up and walls seven feet thick. Its lower chamber can be entered from inside the church through a strong iron grill. There is no east window and the east end looks strangely dark. Windows were inserted in the chancel by public subscription in 1897 to mark the Diamond Jubilee of Queen Victoria, and almost all the stained glass is of the same date. Two of the five windows on the south side are of particular interest. They are beside each other and depict King Edward I, with a view of Burgh church, and St. Kentigern with St. Asaph Cathedral. The blind poet, John Stagg (1770–1823), was born at Burgh.

The road westward from Burgh runs over the open Solway marshes where the cattle are more hazardous to motorists than the floods about which warning is given. Many kinds of migrant geese use this part of the Solway for short or longer stays, and the long skeins pass overhead at certain times of the year—a sight long remembered. The village of Glasson is the centre of haaf net fishing, the local industry; the men stand in the rising water braced against nets, held like small goals in front of them. When the incoming tide threatens to sweep over them, they grudgingly shift to a position nearer the shore. The nets can almost always be seen propped up alongside the road. This village, too, is on the line of the Roman Wall, and many of the old houses are built of stones from it. The older part of the village seems to be dying on its feet, but new houses have been, and are still being, built. The pub is 'The Highland Laddie Inn'. The Methodist chapel has for the past ten years or so been a private house. The canal cutting passes under the bridge.

The canal was the Port Carlisle canal, and the village is about two miles west of Glasson. It was known as Fisher's Cross, until re-named when the canal boom of the late eighteenth century brought about plans to link Newcastle by canal to the west coast. The only portion of the canal to be opened was from Carlisle to Port Carlisle (March 1823). This meant that people from Carlisle could reach Liverpool by sea in one day. Boats were towed along the canal, reaching Port Carlisle in one hour forty minutes.

Monument showing where Edward I died, at Burgh-by-Sands

Built for defence in 1304, the church at Newton Arlosh has the look of a fortress

Port Carlisle, showing the cutting of the former Carlisle Canal

Dalston is a large, residential village near Carlisle

Caldbeck, showing the fells above where stone was quarried for the motorway

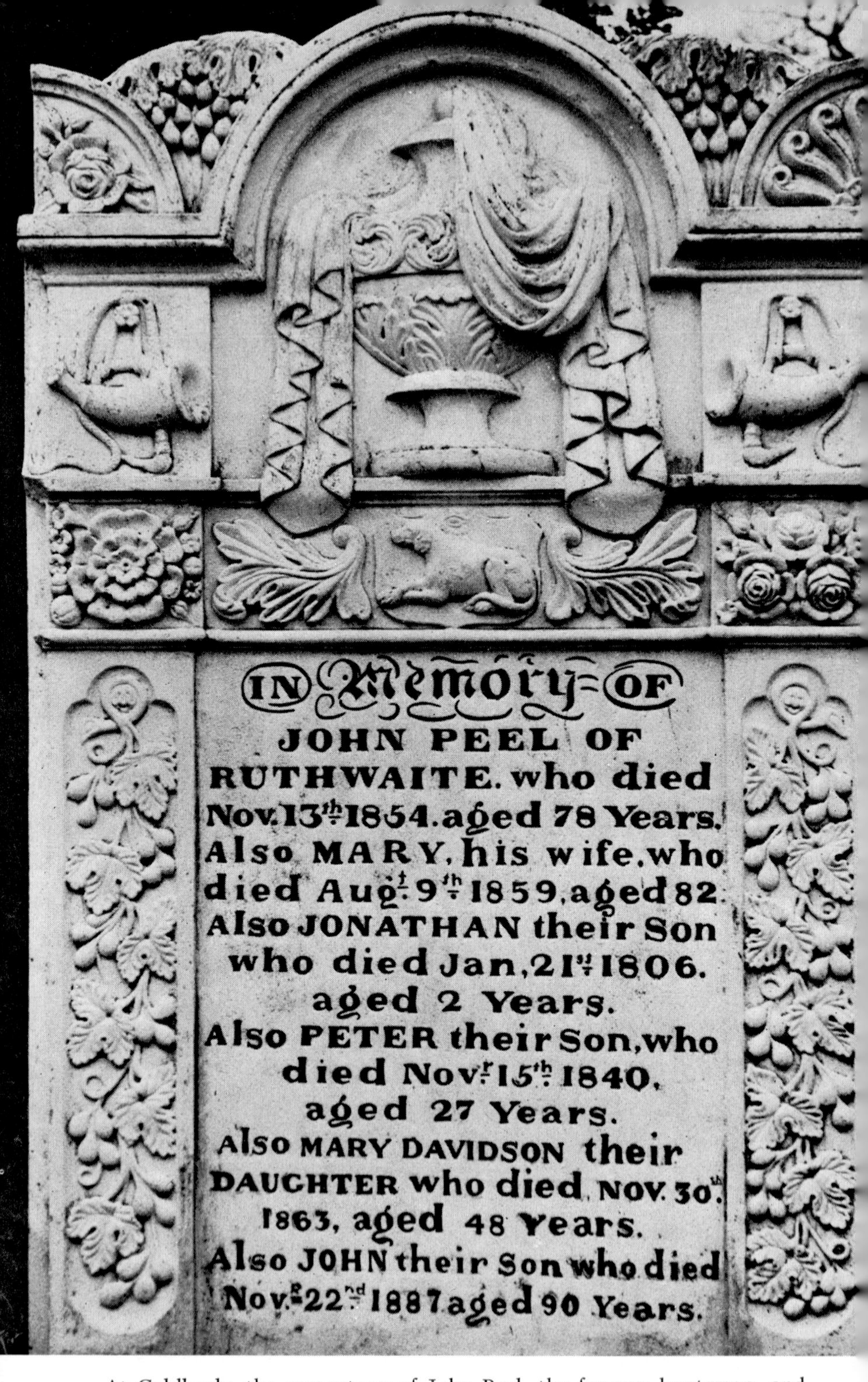

At Caldbeck; the gravestone of John Peel, the famous huntsman, and his wife and children

Passengers then embarked on larger ships which lay waiting in the Solway. By 1829 the canal was becoming uneconomic. It was finally drained in 1853, and replaced by a railway along the canal bed in 1854. The remains of the canal, and the harbour, can still be seen. One house is, in fact, called 'Harbour View'. The village as a whole has a mildly sea-side look about it. There is a Methodist church built in 1861 on the outskirts and a post office-store. The pub is 'The Hope and Anchor Inn'. Above the door of a house at the west end of the village (a house formerly 'The Steam Packet Hotel') is a small, fragmentary Roman altar bearing the words '*Matribus suis milite*'. It will have been dedicated by a contingent of soldiers to the Mother Goddess.

The village of Bowness-on-Solway was built on the westernmost fort of Hadrian's Wall. This meant building material immediately to hand and certainly the church, and some other buildings as well, were built from Roman stones. Some can be easily identified, like the one let in to the wall of a barn on the roadside near 'The Kings Arms Hotel'. It is a small altar from the fort dedicated to Jupiter for the Emperor's well-being. Another particularly interesting stone from the fort is now in Carlisle Museum. It is a trader's vow in verse, hoping for success in his venture. The name Bowness, written in earlier days 'Bulness', indicates a bulge or swelling—a 'rounded headland'. This was the lowest (most westerly) point of the estuary where it was possible to ford the Solway at low water, and the spot was much used as a short cut to Scotland. Presumably for this reason an iron girder viaduct was built a short distance west of the village, linking it by railway with Scotland. This Solway Viaduct was opened in 1869; it was 1,940 yards long. In 1921 it was found to be unsafe and was closed, but was not demolished until 1934–5. A portion of the embankment can still be seen. A modern school is built on to the earlier one of 1875. The post office is opposite the pub. The Wesleyan Home Mission chapel, 1872, is now the Methodist church. The village hall is the Lindow Hall, 1910. St. Michael's church has Norman work in its doorway and a lovely Norman font. This was buried in earlier times in the churchyard, presumably for safety, and was much later in use in a nearby garden as a flowerpot. It was eventually returned to the church in 1848. The windows are interesting. One shows the Archangel Michael standing over a depiction of the church and village (as at Burgh); another shows St. Kentigern and introduces the fish legend (see Introduction, page 16). In the porch are two old bells, marked 1611 and 1616. The story has it that in 1626 some Scotsmen crossed the Solway and stole Bowness church bells. They were spotted and chased and, to lighten their boat, threw the bells into the water. Soon afterwards Bowness men paid a similar visit to Scotland and stole, successfully, the two bells in the porch. The bells were used in the church until 1905 when the present two were given, and the Scottish ones put on display. There was a postcard issued earlier this century depicting the two bells with beside them a piece of verse beginning:

Relieved from duty here we sit
In well-earned ease together,
Beside the Solway's ruddy sands
Secure from wind and weather.
With near three hundred years of toil
A trifle thin our tone is,
So now at length we take our rest—
The stolen Bells of Bowness.

From Bowness the road runs parallel with the Solway coast. Along this stretch some years ago I saw the only viper I have seen in this part of England. Cardurnock, 'the fort in a pebbly place', is only a small group of houses and farms, one dated 1758, hardly worthy of the title of village. Hutchinson says of it that it is 'almost environed by the sea and morasses', and so dangerous from the shifting sands, that 'no traveller or even inhabitant can pass with certainty at all times'. The road from Cardurnock continuing round the headland has only been opened up in the last few years. It is now possible to travel along it to Anthorn on the north bank of the flat estuary of the Wampool where it runs into Moricambe Bay. It was in this spot that the collared dove first bred in Cumbria. The bird was first found breeding in Norfolk in 1955 and expanded its habitat quickly, being first noted at Anthorn in the spring of 1959. The Solway area is now a popular breeding place for the species.

The village of Anthorn—the name means 'the single thorn bush' —is divided into two, the old part and the new. Between them is the Congregational chapel built in 1869. This was re-opened in 1972 as St. Michael's Roman Catholic church to serve Bowness, Glasson, Port Carlisle and Kirkbride. The old village, certainly dating back to 1279, is dominated by the masts and wires of the N.A.T.O. Radio Station opened in November 1964 on the site of the former Royal Naval Air Station (H.M.S. *Nuthatch*) which closed in 1957. According to the histories, and the Ordnance Survey maps, there should be a very ancient cross at the west end of this part of the village. Either it is completely hidden in the gorse, or it was washed away during one of the recurring floods, for it is not to be seen. The newer part of Anthorn has the post office and store, and the community centre. Both parts are plagued by midges.

Moorhouse is a village mainly of recent bungalows, strung along the B5307 road. The pub is 'The Royal Oak'. One house dated 1706 must have been there when Bonnie Prince Charlie's main army spent the night at Moorhouse after crossing the Eden from Rockcliffe, and before starting their siege of Carlisle. A little farther along the road is Thurstonfield. It has a small Methodist chapel of 1861 up a short lane leading south from the road. Beyond it lies Thurstonfield Lough with its variety of waterfowl. The lake used to be frequented by otters, and from time immemorial Carlisle people have skated on it during hard winters. Thurstonfield is now virtually connected by new houses with Kirkbampton, a pleasant village with a post office-store, a fairly recent school and a filling station. The pub is 'The Rose and Crown'. Behind it is St. Peter's church, of ancient foundation, restored in 1882. Parts are Norman, and let into the chancel wall is an even older stone, a Legionary stone from the Roman wall. The doorway is Norman with, on the tympanum above it, a worn figure holding a crook. An even more lovely Norman arch opens into the long, dim chancel. In the chancel is a window of St. Peter. The church has a twin bell-cote with only one bell. A memorial to the fallen in both World Wars is in the churchyard. Two interesting stories are connected with the village. A villager called Hody discovered sleeping in a field a notorious moss-trooper, one of the hated raiders who ravaged England and Scotland alike. Drawing the raider's sword softly from its scabbard he cut off his head. The dead man was buried in Kirkbampton churchyard. The other story is of a former incumbent, Thomas Story, who is recorded as having, before he himself died in 1739, buried every man, woman and child who was living in the parish when he took it over in 1679.

A village on the south bank of the mouth of the river Wampool, and with its Norman church looking out over the marshes towards Moricambe Bay, is Kirkbride. It is spread out along the Wigton road and the B5307. Its pub is 'The Bush Inn'. One house is dated 1721. It possesses stores, two filling stations and a red brick school dated 1875. The Wesleyan chapel, 1869, and the Wesleyan Jubilee Sunday School, 1887, are now the Methodist church. The Primitive Methodist chapel, 1865, rebuilt in 1906, on the other hand, is now a private house. There is a village hall. The church, as the name of the village implies, is dedicated to St. Bride, or more correctly St. Bridget. There was a close link at one time between west Cumberland and Ireland. The hill on which the church stands was a large Roman military site. The chancel arch is Norman and there is a good deal of other Norman work. Sculptures of the birth of Christ, the crucifixion, and the entombment, hang in the arch. Beyond the dim chancel in the east window are depictions of St. Bridget, St. Patrick (whose shroud she wove), and St. Columba. A poignant memorial in the sanctuary tells of the son of a former vicar who, at sixteen and as a midshipman in H.M.S. *Aeolus*, died in 1808. The ancient font has a modern cover given by the Sunday School children in 1933. The holy water trough in the chancel was found in the rectory garden. The old rectory was burned down in March 1960.

A pleasant winding road leads across flat country to Newton Arlosh, sometimes known as Long Newton. It was the 'new town' founded after Skinburness was washed away in 1301, and the inhabitants moved to a safer spot. It is a scattered village now containing old and recent houses, bungalows and farms. The pub is 'The Joiners Arms'. The post office is a private house. There is a village hall, dated 1899, and a school on the outskirts of the village was first built in 1868 and added to later. The church was founded by the abbot of Holme Cultram Abbey, who obtained a charter from Edward I, and was built in 1304. The tower, on the south-west corner, was built for defence and has no outer doorway. The whole church looks rather like a fortress guarding the Solway at Moricambe Bay. The windows are high and narrow. Even the door is narrow. The church is dedicated to St. John the Baptist and in Catholic times it was the parish church for Abbey Town. After the Dissolution, the Abbey church was made parochial and this church became ruinous. It was restored in 1844, and again in 1894. Inside it is very plain and simple, with no stained glass. The altar is at the north end. Two ram's heads in stone stick out of the east wall. The most impressive item is a very finely carved eagle lectern which stands on a base made of bog-oak found in the nearby marshes. The font looks ancient. An unusual sop to creature comfort, tubular electric heaters are fitted along the length of every pew.

Abbey Town is the village of Holme Cultram. It is a hotch-potch of a village with little character, probably from being situated on the main Silloth road. A housing estate is beside the ancient Abbey, yet the post office is a private house opposite 'The Wheat-sheaf Inn', and there are probably more garages than shops. The 1853 school is on the main road and has a prominent clock and a single bell-cote with bell. There is a large and ugly village hall, and a Methodist chapel, originally the Wesleyan chapel, 1859, with the war memorial outside it. The church, of St. Mary, is made from what was once the nave of the Cistercian Abbey of Holme Cultram, founded in 1150 by the son of King David of Scotland at a time when Cumberland was under Scottish rule. The first monks came from Melrose. Rather ironically it is said to have been left standing because the people begged Thomas Cromwell to leave it as a defence for them against the Scots. In 1553 the Abbey was given to Oxford University and about that time or a little earlier (some say 1538) it became the parish church, being, as the inhabitants petitioned, more central than Newton Arlosh church. In 1601 the tower collapsed and much of the Abbey fell into ruins through neglect and decay. The church was restored in 1883 and Holme Cultram is one of the very few Cistercian abbey churches still in use. The west doorway is a magnificent piece of

Norman architecture sixteen feet high. The porch was built by Abbot Chambers between 1507 and 1518. Part of his tomb is preserved; it shows him mitred and robed, surrounded by praying monks, and with the 'chained bear' he used as a pun on his name. The porch is being extended as a museum; another tombstone in it is of Robert the Bruce's father who was buried there in 1294. Bruce himself pillaged the Abbey. The village now runs an Arts Festival connected with the church, where works of art are displayed. Of interest is a brass plate to Joseph Mann of nearby Raby who invented, in Holme Cultram in 1826, the forerunner of the reaping machine.

In the eleventh and twelfth centuries Skinburness was the principal place in the area. It was privileged with fairs and a market, and Edward I used its port facilities for landing the stores for his army engaged in the Scottish wars. Today the village is known chiefly because of its nearness to Silloth and because of the popularity of its hotel. It is loved as a quiet holiday resort, with its one small village store. From the bleak, desolate marshes the old cottages look trimly-painted and inviting. From the sea and Silloth side the village is all recent residential development. On a calm day it is difficult to realize that in 1301 or 1302 a furious storm broke down the sea dyke and the place was swept away in its entirety. In his novel *Redgauntlet* Sir Walter Scott sets the scene of a surreptitious landing by Bonnie Prince Charlie, years after Culloden, at Skinburness where he meets a gathering of Jacobites at an inn with a quay. This inn became a smuggler's clearing-house and local people speak of an underground tunnel connecting it with Abbey Town and Newton Arlosh. It was later known as 'The Greyhound Inn' and as recently as 1933 was divided into several houses. The building still stands on the sea front. The name Skinburness means 'the headland of the demon-haunted castle' and an American professor published a paper claiming that Grune Point is the spot where Sir Gawain, of King Arthur's Round Table, had his fateful meeting with the Green Knight.

Mawbray is a village set at right angles to the Silloth–Allonby road. Many of the houses are at right angles to the by-road and are, therefore, parallel with the sea. A number of them are white-washed. The pub is 'The Lowther Arms Inn' and has mounting steps outside it. There is a post office-store, and a Wesleyan Methodist chapel dated 1843. The school and the church are at Holme St. Cuthbert just over a mile eastwards. This place is sometimes referred to as Rowks, presumably from a chapel of St. Roche which once stood there. The present church, dedicated to St. Cuthbert, was consecrated in 1845 and was restored in 1892. The tower on the west end was built in 1924 to replace a small spire erected in 1877 but found to be unsafe, and removed, in 1919. It is a plain and simple but pleasant and obviously cared-for church. A large crucifix hangs from the chancel arch. There are memorial tablets to the fallen in both World Wars. Of much interest is part of a stone effigy of a warrior found at the beginning of the century. One theory is that it represents the Robert Bruce who is buried at Holme Cultram Abbey. The school at the entrance to the churchyard was built in 1873. Beside it is a small garage-type building bought with the hearse in 1877 "for the use of all the inhabitants".

The small sea-side resort of Allonby, 'Aleyn's settlement', was a sea-side resort with sea bathing as early as 1748. The first church was built in 1744 and there is a record that "on Sunday, the 25th ult. [August 1799] there was one of the most numerous and genteel congregations at Allonby Chapel that has been seen there for many years past, amongst whom were several of the principal gentry of the country. Immediately after divine service the clerk gave notice 'that there would be a horse race at Allonby on the Tuesday following'." This custom of announcing race meetings at the church continued in Cumberland and Westmorland until the middle of last century. Sea Water Baths were erected in 1835, but later became a house. Charles Dickens visited Allonby in 1857. The present church, Christ Church, was built in 1845 on the site of the older church. It is almost as ugly inside as it is outside. It has box pews. The only item of note is a monument with a carved portrait of Captain Joseph Huddart (1741–1816) the navigator, who was born at Allonby, and is buried at St. Martin-in-the-Fields, London. He charted much of 'the Eastern seas' and introduced improvements for the safety of ships.

The building adjoining the church was a school, re-built in 1837. On the whole Allonby is a village which tries to remain 'quaint' and yet also attract holidaymakers. To some extent it succeeds. Many of the houses are painted; one is dated 1666. There is a post office, several shops, and three hotels—'The Grapes Hotel', 'The Solway Hotel', and 'The Ship Hotel'. A riding school is popular. There is a meeting place of the Society of Friends, a Congregational chapel (1844), a Mission Hall, and a village (church) hall dated 1905. An odd-looking building, with a clock-tower, standing on its own represents an attempt to found a reading room and library in 1862. It flourished for forty years or so.

The dunes around Allonby are protected from wind erosion by their natural vegetation.

Crosscanonby is a small, compact village overlooking the Solway. Its name indicates that there was once a convent of canons, doubtless an offshoot of the Augustinian Canons at Carlisle, now of course the Cathedral. What remains today is an absolute gem of a Norman church, dedicated to St. John the Evangelist. Restoration work was carried out in 1880, but more careful and loving restoration has been continued since. For example, the minstrels' gallery with its 1730 carved oak was restored in 1935. The Royal Arms are of George II. The chancel arch is taken from the Roman camp at Maryport and has in it two niches which would in Roman times have held statues, one of the Emperor of the day and the other probably of the commandant's own favourite god. The unusual square alabaster font supported by five columns is ancient. There are many other carved stones.

Baldwinholme, 'Baldwine's piece of land', is just off the main Carlisle to Wigton road. It is a quiet village of new bungalows and old farms. Quiet, that is, from a traffic point of view, for one can usually hear the dogs barking in a well-established boarding kennels there.

Nearby Great Orton is quite a large, mixed village. Its pub, 'The Wellington Inn', is on the outskirts. There is a school, originally built in 1859, and a post office-shop. It is recorded that the village entrances were closed by chains, fastened across them at night. The claim that this was to stop marauding Scots or moss-troopers seems unlikely, and it may well have been quite simply to prevent cattle from straying. The inhabitants say that fifteen churches can be seen and counted in England and Scotland from a field beside the village. For me it was sufficient to see their own church, one of the most delightful small churches I know. It is ancient, dedicated in the late eleventh or early twelfth century. To which saint it was dedicated was disputed until the beginning of the present century, when it was accepted as being to the French saint St. Giles. It is the only church in the Carlisle Diocese so dedicated. There is a window given in 1955 depicting the Saint with a white doe. The legend is that the doe fled to him for protection when being hunted by a party led by King Flavius. An arrow shot at the doe pierced the Saint's protecting hand. The King apologized, and later was induced to found a monastery. St. Giles is, of course, the patron saint of cripples—his church in Cripplegate, London, is well known.

Another interesting window shows St. Kentigern 'Christianizing Cumbria' in A.D. 590. The Sunday School, dating from 1699, was incorporated into the west end of the church in 1868. The marble mosaic work forming the base of the altar was designed by the vicar at the beginning of this century. The carved font-cover carries the Greek palindrome meaning 'Wash not only my face but my sins'. In the churchyard is the tombstone of Richard Dixon, the schoolmaster, who died in 1811 aged sixty-eight. It carries an inscription by a few of his pupils beginning:

> Seven times seven years he taught this school,
> And canvassed many a tedious rule:
> Five times seven years, as you may mark,
> He served here as parish clerk.

William Nicolson (1655–1727), later to become Bishop of Carlisle, was born at Great Orton, literally in the church porch—obviously destined for the religious life!

Wiggonby is a very spread-out village with some large farms. Its chief interest lies in its Endowed School founded by Margaret Hodgson in 1792. She died ten years later and is buried in the churchyard of nearby Aikton. She assigned land and property for the benefit of the school; School Farm is still part of this property. One condition was that all persons of the name of Hodgson, 'without limitation of time or locality', should be educated free of charge. A later school built in 1860 had stables provided for the use of pupils who had to ride in from a distance. The endowment has been taken over by the present school, 1901, but the provision of Easter clothing and the payment for attendance have ceased, the money being paid out in prizes and scholarships. The school at Biglands closed, and was incorporated with Wiggonby school in 1959.

Another spread-out village is Aikton, 'the place of oaks'. Joan de Morville lived at the manor in early days. Her father, Hugh, was one of the assassins of Thomas à Becket (see King's Meaburn in Chapter 4). The pub is 'The Joiners Arms Inn' but earlier this century the village had a hotel run on temperance principles and appropriately called 'The Stingless Cup'. The post office is a private house. The church, dedicated to St. Andrew, is set amongst pleasant fields a short distance from the village. It is a small stone church with a twin bell-cote and two bells, and was restored in 1869. Its chancel arch is almost certainly Norman. The roof beams look old. The south aisle, where the chapel is said to have belonged to the Morvilles, has a fine fourteenth-century piscina. The pulpit carries a date, 1861, but could be older. There is no stained glass. In the churchyard is the well-maintained tomb of Margaret Hodgson who founded and endowed Wiggonby school; and also the memorial to the men who fell in the 1914–18 war, with a steel helmet and sword carved on it.

Oulton is an old village with quite a lot of new housing going up. It is not far from Wigton where presumably many of the people will work. The school was built in 1875 with a single bell-cote and bell. Church of England services used to be held in it occasionally. Extensions were added to it to form the present school. There is a Parish Institute dated 1924. The post office is a private house. A Baptist chapel was built in 1722 and rebuilt as a Primitive Methodist chapel in 1832. It was then given an endowment on condition that a service should be held in it once a month, and be attended by at least three Baptists. By 1900 there had been no Baptists for many years and the chapel was entirely Methodist. Whether the Methodists in their turn have ceased to exist in the area I do not know, but the chapel is now ruinous. The earliest dated cottage seems to be 1818.

There is little to be seen of Dundraw which lies off the Wigton to Silloth road. It has a village institute, and a mission hall dated 1898, which appear to serve the people over a widely scattered area around. One cottage is dated 1730.

Waverton is spoilt by being on the main road from Wigton to Maryport. It has a post office-store and a village hall. East of the village at the crossroads is the plain, unpretentious Church of Christ, built in 1863 as a chapel-of-ease to Wigton. It possesses a single bell-cote and bell, and has a memorial to the fallen in both world wars in its churchyard.

Bromfield, 'broom-covered land', is hardly a village, but it has at least a pub and a church. The pub, dated 1720, is 'Ye Olde Greyhound Inn'. The church is an important one, part Norman, but restored in 1860. It is dedicated to St. Mungo, the affectionate name for St. Kentigern. There have been five churches on the site —a very early, second-century British one, replaced by the Romans who left in A.D. 449; a new church when St. Kentigern ministered there; the Norman church, and the present one. The font is Norman, as are some of the gravestones. The Norman porch has a tympanum of a chequered pattern. On the south wall a sundial is dated 1687. The chancel arch is supported on one side by the head of a Roman monk and on the other that of a Celt, perhaps to symbolize the union of the two Christianities. On the north side is the Lady Chapel re-built in 1860 and containing the tomb of the warrior Adam Crookdale, 1304. On the south side is the chapel of St. George the Martyr, restored in 1925. In the chancel is a recess with the marble figures of two little boys, twins, who died only a few hours after their birth in 1838. A well in a field north of the church is known as St. Mungo's well, and it may have been the spot where St. Kentigern baptized his converts. A more interesting record of the Saint, if one authority is to be believed, is a medallion at the top of the west window. This, according to the Rev. Lees, depicts the head of St. Kentigern with the chin supported by a cloth. I am not convinced of this; but certainly the Saint lived to such an age that his jaw muscles weakened so that he could neither masticate his food nor keep his mouth closed without assistance.

Just beyond the churchyard to the west is the old school building founded in 1612 by Richard Osmotherley, a London merchant who was born at Bromfield. The Cumbrian custom to 'bar out the master' at the beginning of Lent was carried on until 1774. This barring out of the master was a fairly common local custom in these parts where the boys would lock themselves in the school and try to prevent the master from getting in. The siege could last for up to three days, and if the master still failed to obtain admission he had to agree to certain conditions imposed by the boys. The school was re-built and enlarged in 1861. It is now a paint store. Cockfighting used to be very popular at Bromfield and was at one time held in the churchyard, as the vicar was a keen supporter. Jonathan Boucher (1738–1804), a friend of George Washington, was born at nearby Blencogo. He did much of the work for Hutchinson's *History of the County of Cumberland*, 1794. The big-game hunter John Todd (1863–1954) was born and lived at Bromfield.

On the Allonby road is West Newton, a long and pleasant village with not much new building. Until 1857 the villagers worshipped at Bromfield but in that year their own church of St. Matthew was consecrated. It is very typical of the period, with little attractive about it. I think its reredos frankly horrid. St. Matthew's National School nearby was built the following year and opposite the school are St. Matthew's cottages. The pub is 'The Swan Inn'. There is a post office-store and a village hall dated 1952. One cottage dates from 1672. Part of the village is reached across a small stream crossed by bridges.

Rather similar in lay-out to West Newton is the nearby village of Hayton. Its houses, farms, 'The Sun Inn', and the church surround a long, wide village green and street. There is a village hall. The post office is a private house. The 1844 Congregational chapel is now a dairyman's private garage; it still carries a plaque inscribed 'Faith cometh by hearing' on its wall. The church of St. James was built in 1867. Its entrance is dark with trees, and it has a single bell-cote with bell. Heads are carved at each side of the outside windows. Inside is much dark stained glass typical of the period, including a window in the west end based on Holman Hunt's *Light of the World*. The 1899 pulpit was carved by a woman in memory of her father. At the north end of the village is Hayton Castle, now a farm. This was besieged by Cromwell's soldiers during the Civil War when it was the home of the Musgrave family. One of them, Sir Thomas (1737–1812) was the last British Commandant of New York, and fought in the American War of Independence.

Crosby is a large village on the main Maryport road, A596, with a spacious village green. It has houses dated 1724 and 1743 but much of it comprises recent domestic building. Mining was formerly one of its major industries, a pit having been sunk in 1856. It has a post office-store, a school (first built in 1861), a village hall, and a Primitive Methodist chapel (1863). There are three pubs—'The Crown Inn' at one end turning its back on the main road, 'The Sun Inn' at the other end, and 'The Stag Inn' between them.

6

Around the Bishop's Castle

THE villages in the triangle Carlisle, Wigton, Penrith, lie for the most part on the fertile Carlisle plain. Almost in the centre of the triangle, and standing quite on its own away from any village, is Rose Castle, the residence since the thirteenth century of the Bishops of Carlisle. The headquarters of King Edward I, it was sacked by Robert the Bruce. Warwick 'the King Maker' occupied it. It was used as a prison for Royalists in the seventeenth century; one hundred years later the Highlanders went to plunder it but, discovering that the Bishop's infant grand-daughter was about to be baptized, Captain Macdonald chivalrously withdrew, leaving his white cockade for the child to wear. It is not surprising that several of the villages mentioned in this chapter have memorials of some kind to different Bishops.

Just outside the Carlisle city boundary is Cummersdale, 'the valley of the Cumbrians'. It is in fact separated from the city only by the cemetery, the crematorium and the large and modern factory of Pirelli. As one would expect, the fairly large village is mainly residential and for the most part recent. From it one can see the expanding suburbs of Carlisle creeping inexorably outward, maybe one day to engulf it. There is a village hall, a post office-store, and an ugly little church, a daughter church of St. James's, Carlisle, dedicated to the same saint in 1951. The school was founded in 1884. 'The Spinners Arms' is an indication of the textile trade which sprang up in Low Cummersdale very soon after the 1745 Rebellion. The firm of Stead McAlpin, who moved to Cummersdale in 1835 from Wigton, became one of the leading block-printers in the country and early hand blocks of theirs are preserved in Carlisle Museum.

Dalston Hall, in part fifteenth-century, is on the outskirts of Dalston, a large residential village which acts as a dormitory suburb to Carlisle, although local employment is provided by a Nestlé's factory. Near the large new comprehensive school is the old National School, 1864, now the Church of England School. The 1969 telephone exchange is beside the railway station. The Wesleyan Methodist chapel of 1851 was enlarged in 1903 to be the United Methodist Free church. It is now the Methodist church. An octagonal seat on the village green was put there to commemorate the coronation of King George V. The red-flowering chestnut tree was Dalston's prize for gaining third place in the Best Kept Village competition; it won the Award in 1972. The village hall is the Victory Hall, 1922. 'The Blue Bell Inn' and several small shops and stores, including the post office, flank the area in front of the church. A nearby cottage is dated 1690. A market cross used to stand at the east end of the village but was removed in 1815. The red sandstone church, with bell tower and twin bells, is dedicated to St. Michael. A modern lych-gate in memory of a former vicar leads into the churchyard. There are the graves of two Bishops of Carlisle—Edward Rainbowe (1608–84) and Hugh Percy (1784–1856). In the porch are ancient stones and what may have been a very unworthy font. A church has existed since the thirteenth century, but the present one was built in 1750 and restored in 1890. A small window in the west end is to Hugh de Lilford, a hermit who once lived in the parish. Near it is the font, the cover of which was designed by Sir Robert Lorimer (1864–1929), and has representations of the four elements—earth, air, water and fire. These merit close study. The carved and painted reredos and the altar, with its pictures of the Nativity, the Baptism of Jesus, and the Annunciation, are in commemoration of Queen Victoria's Diamond Jubilee, 1897. Along the south wall inside the church runs a seat provided originally for the aged and infirm, in the days when there was no other seating in churches, the congregation either standing or kneeling. The saying about the weak going to the wall probably stems from this amenity. The marble monument to the Reverend Mr. Fletcher is by the local sculptor Musgrave Lewthwaite Watson (1804–47), who carved amongst other works one of the reliefs on the pedestal of Nelson's Column in London.

Almost a part of Dalston is Buckabank, a small village with much recent residential development. It lies on both banks of the river Caldew, whose water was found to be excellent for the manufacture of textiles. Cotton manufacturing was introduced into the village as early as 1780. There is a house dated 1795.

Gatesgill is a small place of farms and houses along the side of Roe Beck. It has a village hall, 1885, and a pub—'The Royal Oak'. Its church is at Raughton Head, a small village with little else but a telephone kiosk, a pillar box and a few whitewashed farms. The church, though, is fairly large and well-kept. Until 1828 the village was in the parish of Dalston but there had been an earlier chapel. The present pulpit is made from a panel dated 1628, taken from the chapel, which is believed to have been thatched with fern. It was re-built in 1678 and restored in 1760 and again in 1881, when a gallery was removed and the tower built. Until 1936 the church had no name, but it was dedicated then to All Saints. The east window (1887) is effective, with the figures enhanced by being partly outlined in clear glass. It was installed by a daughter of Bishop Goodwin. Another window is in memory of Bishop Bardsley (1835–1904), who is buried in the churchyard. The monument to the Reverend Robert Monkhouse, who died in 1822, showing him sitting head in hand, is by Musgrave Lewthwaite Watson, and was his first work in marble; he had been Monkhouse's pupil as a boy. Near the south-east corner of the church is the grave of Susanna Blamire (1747–94), the Cumberland poetess. There is a good view of Rose Castle from the church. From Raughton came Master Ivo, the mason in charge of work at York Minster in 1331, and the craftsman who designed the wonderful east window of Carlisle Cathedral and the similar west window at York. The school near the church was first established in 1744, but replaced by a larger building in 1857.

Cumdivock, 'black valley', is a straggling village with its houses all on the north side of the road. One of them has a 1759 sundial above its door. The Celtic 'cum' in the name, like the Welsh 'cwm',

The eighteenth-century market cross at Hesket Newmarket

The old footbridge at Ivegill. The village is well known for its herb farm

(*below*) John Dalton, the discoverer of the atomic theory, is commemorated at Eaglesfield where he was born

(*right*) The 'Adam' stone at Dearham church is over 1,000 years old

The Wesleyan Methodist chapel at Distington, built in 1830

The terminus of the fifteen-inch gauge Ravenglass and Eskdale railway which was taken over by a preservation society in 1961

stands for 'valley' and has given rise to the local song about places in the county beginning with 'Cum':

> There's Cumwhitton, Cumwhinton, Cumranton,
> Cumrangen, Cumrew, and Cumratch,
> And mony mair cums i' the county,
> But none with Cumdivock can match.

The church lies a little to the west of the houses. Two tall yew trees separate the 1906 lych-gate from the church. The tall 1914–18 war memorial stands in the churchyard, at the west end. The church is a daughter church to Dalston and is dedicated to St. John the Evangelist. It was built in 1871–2 and is a plain church with a belfry and wheel bell. It has stained glass in its east window only. The nearby quarries on the banks of Chalk Beck provided stone for part of the Roman Wall and for Rose Castle and Carlisle Cathedral. At Cardew Hall to the north Susanna Blamire was born.

A village with its green between the busy junction of the Cockermouth, A595, and Maryport, A596, roads is Thursby. It has of recent years grown into a very large residential village, partly because of its nearness to Carlisle. It has a sundial dated 1834 above its bus shelter. Nearby is 'The Ship Inn'. It is claimed that there have been three churches: a wooden one at the time of St. Kentigern's visit to Cumberland; a stone one built about 1124, sold to the then Priory of Carlisle about 1500 and demolished in 1836; and the present one built in 1846. The present church, with its tall tower, is dedicated to St. Andrew. It had new pews in 1878. The pulpit came from Carlisle Cathedral at that time, and was then about one hundred years old. On display in a case is some pewter made in Newcastle and dating from 1750–60. Several members of the Brisco family are buried in their chapel in the south aisle. A large parish hall is near the church. Perhaps the most famous native of Thursby is Sir Thomas Bouch (1822–80) who built the ill-fated Tay Bridge which was swept away in a gale in 1879, carrying a train and all its passengers with it. He also helped with London's first tramway system and the first train ferry across the Forth.

The village of Westward comprises a few old, stone-built houses and farms on a hill above the Wiza Beck. The name indicates that it was the western ward, or division, of the Inglewood Forest. In early Norman times a hermit is said to have lived in this part of the forest and to have dedicated his cell to St. Hilda. The monks of Holme Cultram built a chapel, or oratory, near the spot, and this was the origin of the present church, which was restored and completely transformed in 1879. The entrance, at the west end under a small tower with a pointed spire, has a crude painting of St. Hilda. In the porch is an interesting brass plate to Richard Barwise who died in 1648. After the great siege of Carlisle during the Civil War the city's mayor was 'cast forth by Parliament for his delinquency' and Richard Barwise was ordered to take the office. He was a man of exceptional physical strength and is reputed to have captured two highwaymen at an inn by bending a long poker round both their necks. The church consists of one oblong building, with a flat wooden ceiling. The 1885 east window and one in the south wall, 1896, are the only stained glass, typical of the period. Tablets to the men who gave their lives in both World Wars face each other. The churchyard gates are also in memory of the fallen in the 1914–18 war. The school next to the church 'built by subscription A.D. 1828' has been added to since then.

Rosley, 'where horses grazed', is a tiny village of old houses and farms (one dated 1680) with a little recent development. 'The Hope and Anchor Inn' is on the road to the church, which is some mile and a half north of the village, between Rosley and Woodside. It is a chapel-of-ease to Westward and, like that church, the entrance is at the west and under a tower and small spire. It is dedicated to the Holy Trinity and was built in 1840. The pews are converted box pews. The sanctuary is a recess in the oblong body. There is stained glass, not very good, in the east window (1909) and the windows in the south wall. It is said that when the tower was being built a workman fell off and was killed. The new school (1961) is opposite the church. Horse races used to be held at Rosley, and in July 1829 a Mr. Carruthers challenged the famous John Peel for a stake of ten guineas. I have not been able to find out whether the challenge was accepted. Horse and cattle fairs were held until the beginning of the 1939–45 war, and only legally abolished in 1969.

Old and new houses spread round a large village green with a tall maypole at Welton, a 'place by a spring'. 'The Royal Oak' inn is dated 1770, and a house near the Methodist church is dated 1665. The Anglican church of St. James is a daughter church of Sebergham. It is a plain little church, outside and inside, built in 1872–4, and has a single bell-cote on the slope of the roof. The 1914–18 War Memorial is just outside the porch. There is no stained glass. An odd sort of fretwork and carving of the Lord's Prayer hangs beside the organ. The alms dish has Adam and Eve on it. The new school (1968) is on the outskirts of the village.

Sebergham is a large but scattered village, mainly of farms. One lovely farm house is dated 1730, another house 1769. There is a village hall on the Penrith road and a parish hall, and also the post office, near the church at Churchtown. The village and church are supposed to have been originated, like Westward, by a hermit. In this case William Wastell and his associates set about making a clearing which became the village, and his cell and chapel became the church, on the same site. The lancet window in the nave, now filled with modern stained glass depicting the Good Samaritan, is from the early church and is about 700 years old. There was probably a fortified tower at the west end, where now steps lead up to a door in the 1825 tower. When this present tower was built there was much opposition to it and a rhyme was nailed to the church door beginning:

> The Parson and Miller erected this steeple
> Without the consent or goodwill of the people. . .

During the repairs in 1775 a gallery was added at the west end, to be taken down again at the 1905 restoration. It is a pleasant church dedicated to St. Mary, all of one width, but the roof of the chancel is lower than that of the nave. The baptistry has a recent mosaic of Christ with children. In the sanctuary is a very fine 1616 memorial to Thomas Denton, and also a tablet to the Reverend Josiah Relph (1712–43), the poet, curate and schoolmaster who was born at Sebergham. A work Pevsner calls 'one of the most effective monuments of its time in all England' is on the north wall. It is by the sculptor Musgrave Lewthwaite Watson (1804–47); a memorial to his father who died in 1823. It shows the three Fates in profile, and is copied from Fuseli's *Three Witches* (from *Macbeth*). Watson was born at Sebergham and there is a memorial tablet to him in Carlisle Cathedral. The lych-gate leading into the churchyard is in memory of an officer killed in Mesopotamia in 1916.

Second perhaps to Grasmere in being best-known village in the region is Caldbeck, 'cold brook'. It is an attractive village, but its fame springs almost entirely from one man, John Peel (1776–1854)—although it would be more correct to say two men, and to include John Woodcock Graves, who wrote the words of the song which made the huntsman famous all over the world; although few of the thousands who visit the grave of Peel in the village churchyard each year could tell you whose words they sing. A shelter opposite the church was erected in 1939 in memory of both men. Graves worked in one of the mills that sprang up beside the fast-flowing stream, and produced the 'grey' cloth also made famous in the song. Ruins of the mills still stand west of the village and over the door of one is the date 1671. There are houses dated 1666 and 1718. The pub is the 'Oddfellows Arms Inn'. There is a Wesleyan chapel bearing a plaque 'Remember now thy Creator 1832' which is now the Methodist church. The appearance of the village is marred by overhead power cables, but the Electricity Board has promised to put these underground shortly as part of its amenity scheme. The church is dedicated to St. Kentigern, whose well is nearby to the left of a footbridge over the stream. It is an ancient church, with some Norman remains from the original stone church built in 1118 in connection with a hospice for distressed travellers. Underneath the tower, inside the church, is the statement that 'This Steple was builded in the year 1727' followed by the names of five churchwardens. The clerestory windows, removed at the beginning of last century, were restored in 1933. Modern stained glass in the east window of the north aisle depicts St. Kentigern and St. Patrick. The mid-thirteenth-century tombstone in the sanctuary is of

Thomas de Brey of Kirkby Thore in Westmorland. The Royal Arms are of George IV. The churchyard also contains the grave of Mary Robinson, 'The Beauty of Buttermere', who later married Richard Harrison, Julia Marlowe, the Shakespearian actress who died in 1950, and whose real name was Sarah Frances Frost, was a native of Caldbeck. Stone for the motorway was quarried in the fells above Caldbeck.

Attractive houses surround the long village green of Hesket Newmarket. On the green is the eighteenth-century market cross, consisting of four round pillars with a pyramid roof. It is now more or less absorbed by the buildings of a filling station. The post office-store is in the fine wide main street. So is the pub, 'The Old Crown', with a sign depicting a William and Mary crown piece. The Methodist chapel is opposite. At the west end of the village is Hesket Hall, which is said to have been built in such a way that the shadows cast by the twelve angles and the circular roof indicated the time of day, after the manner of a sundial.

Skelton is quite a large village with a good deal of recent development. It is set on a crossroads, with its neat little village green. The name indicates that it is a 'place on a hill, or bank'. Houses are dated 1714 and 1730. The Primitive Methodist chapel is 1865. There is a 1923 village hall, 'The Dog and Duck Inn', a village store, and a new school. The post office is a private house. The church of St. Michael and All Angels was built when the old one was taken down in 1879. The square, ancient-looking tower has on its south wall a large sundial of the 1750s. It is a low oblong church with a wide low chancel arch. The east window is very ornate. In the past there has been some dispute as to whether the church's dedication is to St. Mary, or to St. Michael. The lych-gate is a 1914–18 War Memorial.

Little and Great Blencow comprise one rather scattered old village. Sixteenth-century Blencow Hall is now a farmhouse. The pub is 'The Crown Inn'. The Wesleyan chapel of 1877 is now the Methodist church. There is a house dated 1769. At one time very important to Blencow was its celebrated Grammar School. Founded in 1577 it continued until 1913, when it merged with Penrith Grammar School. Its founder was Thomas Burbank and his name and the following couplet can still be read with difficulty over a door:

> Ye youthe rejoice at this foundation
> Being made for your good education.
> A.D. 1577.

The building is now a farm, easily identified by its square cupola. Two pupils of the school who became famous were George Whitehead (*c.* 1636–1723), the Quaker; and Edward Law (see page 40).

Taking its name from the de Reigny family who held this part of Cumberland in 1185, is the attractive cluster of old and new houses Newton Reigny. It boasts two pubs, 'The George III Inn' and 'The Sun Inn'. A 1761 lintel is built into an outhouse. The village hall is the Nicholls Memorial Hall, 1912. The post office is a private house. The church, of St. John, has a bell-cote with two bells. It was completely restored in 1891–2 and is a wide low church with north and south aisles. It has no stained glass except for one small modern piece in the sanctuary, representing St. Nicholas of Myra. The beam nearest the chancel has on it writing, difficult to decipher. I understand that it gives the names of two carpenters, John Atkenson and Henere Bymert, who built the roof in 1585.

The fairly large village of Calthwaite is within sight and sound of the motorway. On the whole, the newer houses have been built away from the older ones in the original village. There is a post office-general store, and 'The Globe Inn'. The school, with its bell-tower and bell, was re-built in 1875, and a classroom added for Queen Victoria's Jubilee in 1897. It has since been extended further —extensions which meant demolishing the old cockpit which stood behind the school. The name Calthwaite means 'the meadow where calves were kept' and the village still lives up to its name for it possesses one of the largest Jersey herds in the country. Before the church was built in 1913 divine service was held in the school. The church is simple and fresh inside, its woodwork clean and polished. The only decorations are a small wooden plaque of Dürer's *Hands of an Apostle*, and a carved angel on each side of the sanctuary arch. There is no stained glass. The 1914–18 War Memorial is outside the church.

Ivegill is a small village on the deep cleft of the river Ive, from which it takes its name. The bridge over the river, Wharton Bridge, was opened in May 1924 and near it is the old high-arched footbridge. The village is famous for its herb farm. On the outskirts are the village hall, opened in October 1964, and opposite it the school, adapted and enlarged in 1965 from the 1873 school building which still carries its bell-cote and bell. A chapel-of-ease to Dalston served the villagers from 1338 to 1868 when the present church, Christ Church, was opened. It was built entirely at the cost of the first vicar, the Reverend A. E. Hulton, who saw it consecrated in July 1868 and died two months later. It is a plain, schoolroom-type church, made dark with much stained glass typical of the period. The east window is a representation of the Last Supper, with vines and grapes underneath. This motive is continued in the carved oak reredos. The brass eagle lectern is in memory of a Deputy Consul-General of the Niger Coast Protectorate who 'fell in ambuscade' in 1897.

7

The Coastal Strip from Maryport to Millom

THIS chapter includes those villages which lie between the seashore and the A5086 and A595 roads. It is a long narrow strip of mostly low-lying land, embracing the undoubted ugliness of the industrial belt of West Cumberland in the north, the haunting loneliness of the Drigg Nature Reserve in the middle, and the tired and largely played-out industrial town of Millom in the south. To the east hangs the beautiful back-cloth of the Lake District mountains, often made fanciful as erratic patches of sunshine catch them here and there. It is not always realized that the smaller local authorities are responsible for their own stretches of coastline, although they can get help from the County Council. Nor is it general knowledge that it is illegal to take stones from the beaches for the purpose of building a rock garden.

The large but ugly village of Flimby is separated from the Solway by the main A596 road and the railway. The station is now an unmanned halt, and part of the building has become a private house. Because of the coal which was abundant nearby, the village population grew by eight or nine times during the last century, and the place could now be classed as almost a small town. The pit is closed and filled in. Flimby Lodge, once a girls' boarding school, was converted in 1886 into a school, and into vagrant wards. It is now derelict. There are quite a number of shops and three pubs—'The Miners' Arms' (with an unusually good inn-sign) at one end of the village, 'The Schooner' at the other end, and 'The Princess Royal Inn' set back from the road between them. At the back of the disused Primitive Methodist chapel (1862) and Wesleyan chapel (1872) is the 1927 Miners' Welfare Institute. The Wesley Hall, 1925, is opposite the chapels. The church of St. Nicholas is in the old part of the village away from the coast. It was built in 1794 on the site of the previous church, and was restored in 1862. Its interior was renovated in 1897. It is a plain, simple church with an east window depicting scenes from the life of Christ. A house not far away is dated 1771.

Seaton, 'the place on the sea', is now quite well inland. It also is a large village with much recent residential development. It has two pubs, 'The Coachman Inn' and 'The Royal Oak', a Working Men's Institute (1899), a boys' club, a British Legion club, and a riding school. There is a Wesleyan Methodist church dated 1860 and enlarged in 1906. The Anglican church struck me as surprisingly large. It is dedicated to St. Paul and was built in 1883. The east end is an apse with the only stained glass in its three windows—one of 1905 and the other two 1925. The not very attractive altar frontal is in modern carved light oak.

A sign saying 'steep hills and bends' welcomes the visitor to Camerton. It comes as something of a surprise, after seeing the village so beautifully set in a valley thick with trees, and with a lovely panorama of the Lake hills, to learn that it was built as a mining village. Evidence of this lingers in the reclaimed slag heaps and in the name of one of its pubs, 'The Colliers' Arms'; the other is 'The Railway Inn'. The post office is a private house. Its main feature of interest is its church, and the effigy inside it. The church, of St. Peter, lies some distance from the village, down a rough road and across a field to a bight in the river Derwent. The churchyard gate is in memory of a man who lost his life on board H.M.S. *Thracian* during the 1939–45 war. The war memorial to the dead of both world wars is in the churchyard. The church was first erected in 1000, re-built in 1694, and again in 1796. The tower and spire were added in 1855 and the church thoroughly restored in 1892. Inside is the beautifully preserved effigy in black stone of a knight in full armour, representing Thomas Curwen, known as 'Black Tom', a very famous warrior who died about 1500. Near him hang long-handled collecting shovels.

Built round a cross-roads, and much of it recent and uninspired, is Broughton Moor, at one time locally known as Wyndham Row. This, too, is a village whose inhabitants were mostly employed in the coal mines, and again we have 'The Miners' Arms Inn', as well as 'The Solway Inn'. The Primitive Methodist chapel of 1861 is now closed and replaced by a Methodist church of 1902. There is also a Mission Room. At the beginning of this century the local people took sufficient stone from a local quarry to build a church and vicarage. The quarry was then sealed. The 1904 church is dedicated to St. Columba. It is a plain but attractive little church with a floor which slopes slightly upwards towards the altar. The custom is preserved, when anyone dies, of pushing the coffin on a wheeled bier through the streets from the house to the church, with the funeral procession following.

The much better-known Broughton lies about two miles south-east and comprises Little Broughton and Great Broughton. It is a village made to seem more interesting than it really is by the disorderly lay-out of most of its older houses, many of them opening directly on to the main street. There are several shops as well as the post office-store, and a variety of pubs including 'The Volunteer Inn', 'Brewery House', 'The Punch Bowl Inn' and 'The Sun Dial'. The Wesleyan chapel is dated 1846 and the Primitive Methodist chapel 1869. Christ Church, built in 1856, is reached through a large housing estate. It has a single bell-cote with bell, and its plain interior is topped by a steeply sloping roof. The pulpit is very solid looking. The communion rails came from St. Cuthbert's Church, Seascale. In the eighteenth century almost the entire population of Little Broughton comprised either weavers (a common village occupation) or, much more unusually, tobacco-pipe makers. To one of the latter families was born, in 1714, Abraham Fletcher. His father begrudged him formal education and he had only three weeks at school. He taught himself to read and write, and turned with fascination to arithmetic—doing all this at night, after a hard day's pipe-making. In 1752 he was able to handle with pride the two-volume work he had written: *The Universal Measurer*. He died in 1793, after having been schoolmaster and village doctor.

The hilly little village of Papcastle is so close to Cockermouth as to be almost a suburb of it. Despite a great deal of modern development, the old part of the village is still picturesque, with its houses built on the hillsides. The post office is a private house, and there is a house with a stone dated 1668 in its gable end. Opposite is the old village hall, now a daughter church to Bridekirk. The 1895 reading room is the headquarters of the Women's Institute. Ekwall gives the name as probably meaning 'the Roman fort where the hermit lived', but it may be that it is a contraction of Pipard's Castle.

The manor of Papcastle belonged in early days to Ochtreda, the heiress of the lords of Egremont. It was her son, known as 'The Boy of Egremont', who fell into the Strid near Bolton Abbey and was drowned. He is referred to as 'the noble boy of Egremound' in Wordsworth's poem *The White Doe of Rylstone*. Papcastle passed to his sister who married Gilbert Pipard, one of Henry II's judges. He built a castle, Pipard's Castle, which with the passage of time became Papcastle. An eccentric born at Papcastle about 1697 was Salathiel Court. He was respected as a writing master until he fell into bad company and habits. There are many stories of his original sense of humour. One concerns an inn-sign he was painting for a publican who wanted a lion on it. Court asked if he could paint the lion chained, but his request was refused. He therefore painted the sign in watercolours which, at the first heavy shower, ran, the lion disappearing. It would not have done so, he pointed out, if he could have had it chained! At one period he was a bellman at Whitehaven and drew crowds to listen to his pronouncements, often in verse. He was finally deported to America for celebrating illicit marriages.

The village of Brigham, 'the meadow by the bridge', lies on the opposite side of the A595 to its church. The old part of the village can still be seen along one long main street. There is a Wesleyan chapel dated 1882 which replaced a smaller one of 1856. The village hall is the Memorial Hall, 1924. The post office and 'The Appletree Inn' are in the village, while 'The Wheatsheaf Inn' and 'The Lime Kiln Inn' are on the main road. The church is dedicated to St. Bridget, and is part Norman. It shows a variety of styles and was entirely, but carefully, restored between 1864 and 1876. There is a most unusual and attractively decorated ceiling, and a piscina with faces. The stained glass in the east window is in memory of Wordsworth's son John, who was vicar for many years. On the south side is a window of Adam and Eve. The memorial to the fallen of both world wars is outside the church. George Fox tells in his *Journal* how he went into the church one Sunday afternoon and, standing on a seat, preached to the congregation for three hours. On another occasion he tells of a theological discussion he held with the vicar, Mr. Wilkinson, which went on for so long that the vicar's dinner was spoiled. As a result (of the discussion, not the ruined dinner) Mr. Wilkinson and a great number of his congregation were converted to the Quaker belief.

Great and Little Clifton lie close to each other on the Cockermouth–Workington road. Neither has any claims to beauty. Great Clifton is a shabby place redolent of the coal-mining which was once its main livelihood. Tradition has it that in former times a market was held there, borne out perhaps by the name of the pub, 'The Market Cross'. There is a post office. Little Clifton, slightly more attractive, has a good deal of modern building. Its pub is 'The Greyhound Inn' and it possesses a church, dedicated to St. Luke and perched above the main road almost at the junction with the Whitehaven road. It has a single bell-cote and bell, and appears to be kept locked.

A place which has retained very much of its true village character, although sadly spoilt by overhead power cables, is Greysouthen. Ekwall contends that it is named after a medieval Irishman, Suthan, and means 'Suthan's cliff'. The village hall and the pub, 'The Punch Bowl', are on the main street, but the 1833 Wesleyan chapel is at the end of a side street. It cost £161 when built.

Eaglesfield is a village with a proud place in the worlds of education, science, and the sea. Robert Eglesfield was born in the village, became confessor to Queen Philippa, Edward III's queen, and was also the founder of Queen's College, Oxford, where he was buried in 1349. Another native was Fletcher Christian, born at nearby Moorland Close in 1764 and known to the world for his part in the mutiny on the *Bounty* and the founding of the colony on Pitcairn Island. Most famous, however, was the first developer of the atomic theory, John Dalton. The house where he was born in 1766 may still be seen, with a memorial tablet above the incongruously modern door. He taught in the village school at the age of twelve, but achieved his real fame in Manchester, where he died in 1844. A fact less widely known about Dalton, although he himself wrote about it, is that he was colour-blind. He was born of Quaker parents, and the incidence of colour-blindness is a peculiarity more common amongst that sect than amongst non-Quakers. Whether this is the reason why they customarily wore drab clothing, or whether it came afterwards, is open to speculation. Carlisle Public Library has in its collection a sheet of coloured ribbons indicating how they were seen by Dalton.

Eaglesfield church is some distance from the village close to the A5086 and is called the John Dalton Memorial church. It was erected by the Royal Society to commemorate him. In the village is the Wesleyan chapel dated 1845. The pub is 'The Black Cat Inn' and there is a post office-store.

By a strange coincidence there was born at the vicarage of Dean in 1709 another, though considerably less famous, John Dalton. He was a minor poet who adapted John Milton's *Comus* for the stage, with melodies by Dr. Arne. One performance was given with the famous David Garrick speaking a prologue written by the equally famous Dr. Johnson. This performance was for the benefit of Milton's grand-daughter Elizabeth, whom Dalton had discovered to be in need. Dean is a charming village with both old houses and farms, and quite a lot of recent housing. The pub is 'The Royal Yew' (quite a change from so many 'Royal Oaks') and has a large yew tree in front of it. There is a church hall, and a school with bell-cote and bell. There was once a grammar school, founded as early as 1596, which stood in the present churchyard where the war memorial is today. It continued until 1872 and was demolished in 1893. The churchyard is entered under a lych-gate with seats, put there in 1916. Outside the church is an ancient preaching cross, probably of the twelfth century, with a later stem which carried a sundial. Three original fourteenth- and fifteenth-century gargoyles, one positioned face downwards, decorate the south wall, with a bell-cote and two bells above them. The bell ropes hang down, unusually, into the chancel. The church is dedicated to St. Oswald, King of Northumbria, and much restoration has been carried out since 1955. In 1968 new chancel furniture was added.

The pulpit and lectern have a small mouse carved on them; this is the symbol of the Yorkshire firm of Robert Thompson who made them. Dean means simply a 'valley'.

Branthwaite, the 'broom-covered clearing', is situated on the steep banks of the river Marron. It is a pleasant village of old and new houses on each side of the three roads. There are two pubs, 'The Star Inn' and 'The Wild Duck'. Branthwaite Hall, now a farm, is between the village and Dean. It was, from 1422 to 1757, the home of the Skeltons, the last of whom, General Skelton, left it to Captain James Jones who had saved his life during their service together. William Hetherington (1788–1865), a local poet, lived in the Hall and was buried in Dean churchyard.

What was formerly the small fishing port of Harrington has grown into quite a large place with new housing estates surrounding the old village. High Harrington is almost a community of its own, with a post office, 'The Galloping Horse Inn' and 'The Brewery House Hotel'. The original village has a large Primitive Methodist chapel dated 1891, a Presbyterian church (1881), a school dated 1875 and a post office. It has several inns, including 'The George and Dragon' (with rather a caricature of an inn-sign), 'The Ship Inn', 'The Station Hotel', and 'The Golden Lion Inn'. Ample parking space has been provided by the docks and, if one can ignore the slag heaps, a degree of industrial smoke, and a general air of run-down tiredness, the sea front could be a very pleasant place for a summer afternoon. The harbour was originally constructed in 1760. The church, dedicated to St. Mary, is set in a large, irregularly-shaped churchyard overlooking the old town. It is not a very attractive-looking church (re-built in 1885), and the tower on the west end looks to be separate from the body of the church. It was in fact added in 1905–7. Inside, the church, with a centre aisle only, is long and rather barn-like, but well kept, with something pleasing about its 1912 east window. The north wall has bronze plaques to the fallen of both World Wars and also the remains of old tombstones. There is a twelfth-century font in the porch. A very new church hall has been built close by.

A good deal of industrial development has taken place in and around Distington since it was a village, with the consequent flowering of housing estates, mostly of a quite ugly, drab grey.

The older part lies on one long main street, which also contains the original Wesleyan Methodist chapel dated 1830. There is a Sunday School dated 1836. The 1899 reading room is now a private house. A handful of pubs include 'The Queen's Head', 'The Black Lion', 'The Globe Hotel' and 'The Antelope Inn'. The Church of the Holy Spirit, built in 1886, stands on a hill overlooking the village and surrounding countryside. The chancel arch of the seventeenth-century church stands in the churchyard, and there are believed to have been two earlier churches. It is a lofty church with colourful windows, one of the Passion. It has a pulpit with carvings from the life of Christ, and the pillars are of polished Shap granite. The old font is dated 1662. On the Whitehaven road is a fine war memorial.

Between the sea and the Whitehaven road is the grim, dingy village of Lowca. Its appearance speaks of the mining and slag heaps which surround it. Outside its Methodist church (1910) is the memorial to the fallen in both World Wars. The school is at the top of the hill, and there is a post office-store, a central hall, and 'The Ship Inn'. The lovely church, set in such pit-spoilt surroundings, belongs not to Lowca but to Moresby. Dedicated to St. Bridget, the Irish saint who visited Cumberland in the sixth century, it was built in 1822 but much restored in 1885 and again in 1895 after a fierce gale had wrecked its roof. It was further enlarged in 1901. Though it is plain on the outside, it is a joy to walk inside and admire the carved wooden pulpit, with its painted front, and the interesting stained glass windows. There is a gallery at the west end. In the churchyard is the chancel arch of the earlier church, and between the church and the main road is a field which was the site of an important Roman station. The village of Moresby, or Moresby Parks, is very largely of new and recent residential property. It has a post office and general store, St. Bridget's Mission Church, and a recent Methodist church, St. Mark's. The name Moresby means 'Maurice's place'.

Set between the ugliness of the Marchon Works and the beauty of St. Bees Head, Sandwith has managed to retain something of its village character. Its name means 'sandy ford'. It has a post office and two pubs—'The Lowther Arms' and 'The Dog and Partridge'. There is a house dated 1661. The old school bearing dates for 1834, 1847 and 1906 can still be seen beside the road going towards St. Bees lighthouse. Long before the first lighthouse was built, a beacon fire was burned on the Head to warn and guide shipping. A look-out for enemy ships was also kept in times of war. The first lighthouse was destroyed by fire. The second, built in 1822, was replaced by the present one in 1866–7. The Head is named after the Irish princess, Bega, who founded a nunnery after fleeing to these parts from Ireland to avoid marriage. According to legend she asked for land on which to build her abbey and was laughingly offered as much land as snow would cover on the following morning, Midsummer's Day. Snow fell, and she got her land.

Hensingham, although listed as a village, is now virtually a part of Whitehaven, and there is no longer a village as such. It is, however, worth mentioning the large, light, airy church of St. John the Evangelist, built in 1913, with its interesting picture windows, and the fine oak war memorial with its carving of St. George and the dragon. Edmund Grindal (1519–83) was born at Hensingham. He was Bishop of London when St. Paul's was burnt; and later was Archbishop of York, and then of Canterbury. He founded St. Bees Grammar School, and his name appears in Spenser's *Shepheards Calender* under the anagram of Algrind.

Arlecdon, 'the valley of the eagle stream', sounds more attractive in that description than in Pevsner's words, 'a mining village of no attraction'. Unfortunately Pevsner is right and there is little of merit to see in the village. The post office is one of a row of undistinguished houses. There is a Sunday School dated 1878, and plans being considered for converting it into a community centre. The pub is 'The Sun Inn'. The 1829 church, remodelled in 1904, appears to be kept locked, probably because it is quite isolated. It is dedicated to St. Michael. The churchyard is entered under a lych-gate or by way of a rather peculiar stile built round a drinking fountain (not in use). In the churchyard is the memorial to the dead of both World Wars, and also to a death in 1967. A hundred and sixty years ago there was a regular raceground in the village, with an annual mixed programme.

Almost joined on to, and almost identical with, Arlecdon is Rowrah. It is a long village of uninteresting houses stretched along

The twelfth-century font at Bridekirk Church, one of the finest pieces of Norman sculpture in the country

The main street at Ireby with its market cross. A market charter was first granted in 1237

Bampton village and church. The river is the Lowther.

(*left*) Blindcrake. The stone shows where the village pump once stood
(*right*) The twelfth-century font in Ireby Church

'The Greyhound Hotel' at Shap

This effigy of Robert Southey, Poet Laureate, is in Crosthwaite church. Southey is buried in the churchyard

the A5086. There is a Methodist church and Wesleyan Sunday School dated 1895. The pub is 'The Stork Hotel'. Rowrah Hall Quarry has been worked since 1888. It is a far cry from the days when the name Rowrah stood for 'the nook where rye is grown'.

In this part of the Whitehaven hinterland the villages seem doomed to ugliness. Frizington is a large village, almost a small town, which Pevsner describes as 'a depressing place'. I found it less so than Arlecdon, or Rowrah, or Lowca. It is, of course, another village which could almost be said to owe its existence to mining. There is a good deal of new building in progress. It is interesting that oil was used for the public lighting until the early years of this century. The church, dedicated to St. Paul, was built in 1867–8. It is a plain church with a balcony. The east window depicts scenes from the life of Christ, and brass plates to those who fell in both World Wars face each other on the walls. St. Joseph's Catholic church was built in 1890, after the congregation had worshipped in a small school chapel for about fifteen years. A church hall is now being added beside the church. The new Methodist church, St. John's, is opposite the now disused 1894 building. There is a large Working Men's Club, a Freemasons Hall, a Gospel Hall (1892), and several pubs including 'The Anchor Inn', 'The Griffin', 'The Royal Oak', and 'The Travellers Rest'. The southern part of the village appears to be overdue for demolition.

Cleator Moor is described by Pevsner as 'a drab mining village'. I would rate it as a small town, almost beyond the scope of this book. The church of St. John the Evangelist, consecrated in 1872, appears to be kept locked. A new Roman Catholic church, St. Bega's, was opened in 1970. There is a town hall (1877) and a rectangular market place, and the development of light industries and the housing estates have meant that in little more than a hundred years a small town has appeared where there was virtually nothing before. For in nearby Cleator the older natives remember their grandparents speaking of bare moorland where Cleator Moor now stands.

Cleator itself is vastly different from Cleator Moor, and its main street retains its village character. On the outskirts is the large, fanciful and ornate Roman Catholic church of Our Lady of the Sacred Heart, designed by Pugin in 1853–6. It is said to be on the site of a pre-Reformation chapel. The church contains much rich carving in both wood and stone, the altar piece and reredos being particularly worth notice. In the village are two pubs, 'The Three Tuns' and 'The Millers Inn'. The Wesleyan chapel dated 1862 is closed, and looks dingy. The church of St. Leonard is ancient but, being dilapidated and suffering from dampness, it was completely renovated in 1841; in fact all was rebuilt except the chancel. A fine shelter with seats was built on to the north side during the rebuilding of 1900–3. The font was originally in the old priory church of St. Bees. The stone pulpit projects from a bay in the wall. The stained glass windows are colourful, and include two which are memorials to the 1914–18 war, and one depicting the Lady of Egremont and St. Bega. Opposite the church is the Parish Church Jubilee Room (1899). Cleator means the 'rock or cliff shieling'.

Rather dominated by the cooling towers and chimneys of the Windscale nuclear power station is the pleasant village of Beckermet. It is just off the A595 road, in fact the war memorial to the villagers killed is at the junction of the roads. The village is two villages, in fact; each named after its church—St. John Beckermet and St. Bridget Beckermet. The name indicates 'the junction of two streams', Black Beck and Kirk Beck (hence Kerbeck Stores in the village). The present St. John's church was built in 1878–9 to replace a building demolished in 1810, which must have been an ancient one. There are many old fragments and tombstones in the present church porch and elsewhere. The brick finish inside gives the church a more sombre appearance than it deserves. The carved screen (1920) in the chancel arch is a memorial to the 1914–18 war dead. The altar has a carved frontal of vines. The Royal Arms are of Queen Victoria. A pitch pipe used from 1847 to 1860 is on display. The old font is in the churchyard. There are two pubs, 'The White Mare' and 'The Royal Oak Hotel', and a post office-store. St. Bridget's church was in effect superseded by the church of the same name at Calder Bridge in 1842. The old church still stands, however, with its twin bell-turret, half a mile south-west of Beckermet. It is a very plain little church indeed. Its whitewashed walls lean slightly outwards.

There is no stained glass, nor ornamentation of any kind. The Royal Arms are of George III. The altar is a simple stone slab on four stone legs. The church is still used, but only for funerals and for a few occasional services. There are two very old cross shafts in the churchyard. There is a good antiquarian bookshop in the village.

Calder Bridge is on the main A595 where the river Calder is crossed by a bridge—hence the name. It is a small village with a pub on each side of the bridge; 'The Golden Fleece' and 'The Stanley Arms Hotel'. The latter presumably takes its name from the Stanley family, many of whom are buried in Ponsonby church nearby. There is a post office-store, and the 1894 school is being enlarged. Opposite the church is a house dated 1727. The church is the parish church of St. Bridget Beckermet, and took the place of the old church in Beckermet in 1842. It is a cruciform building of no particular merit. The east window is listed as being on the theme of 'Faith and Love' and was executed in 1894 by Henry Holiday (1839–1927) whose work was noticed at Casterton. It includes a picture of the church itself. In the churchyard is the memorial to both World Wars. Calder Abbey, three-quarters of a mile higher up the Calder, was founded for the Order of Savigny in 1134. The Order united with the Cistercians in 1148. The world's first full-scale nuclear power station lies south-west of Calder Bridge. The Windscale plant for producing plutonium opened in 1951, followed in 1956 by the Calder Hall power station producing electricity.

Now approached through a large modern housing estate, Seascale means 'the hut by the sea'. It is a village which grew in the wake of the coast railway and has developed almost entirely since the middle of the last century. Many of its residents are employed at Calder Hall and Windscale. Its fine open stretches of sand and its golf course make it ideal for family holidays, and there is much accommodation for visitors. One house has a ship's figure-head. There is a Methodist church dated 1887, and a very new Roman Catholic church and hall (St. Joseph's). The Anglican church, dedicated to St. Cuthbert, was consecrated in 1890 as a chapel-of-ease to Gosforth, becoming an independent parish in 1904. Before it was built, services were conducted in the railway station waiting room and goods shed. A corrugated iron church was built on the present site in 1881 but was badly damaged by a storm in 1884. The church has some fine wood carving and a colourful east window (1911). At the back of the altar hangs a replica of St. Cuthbert's Cross in Durham Cathedral, the work of Keswick Industrial Arts. Other St. Cuthbert links are provided by the carvings on the clergy stalls of the otter (depicting the story of the otters who kept the Saint's feet warm as he prayed) and the seagull (representing the seabirds who were his friends). The communion rail in oak is in memory of the men who died in the 1939–45 war. The memorial cross for the 1914–18 war is in the churchyard. The bell-turret has two bells, and the clock on the west front commemorates the coronation in 1937 of George VI.

Drigg is a scattered village set in flat fields. There is an old saying 'Let us gang together like the lads of Drigg and the lasses of Beckermet' referring to a time when the men of Beckermet had been killed in battle and the young men of Drigg were taken and married to the Beckermet women. This gave rise to a rather fanciful idea that the name Drigg came from 'dreg' or 'drag away'. About 1670 Sir William Pennington is recorded as having established a 'horse course' on the sands between the Irt and the sea where horse races were run annually in May. This was presumably in the area which is now a nature reserve. 'The Victoria Hotel' is beside the railway station. There is a village hall, and a school dated 1876, but founded in 1828. An 1887 lych-gate leads into the churchyard, and to the church of St. Peter built in 1850 on the site of an older one. It is a plain, lofty church containing a remarkable tablet to the Reverend William Singleton whom the Almighty suddenly removed 'from Time to Eternity'. There are brass tablets to the fallen of both World Wars, and a window showing Christ healing the sick, dedicated to an Ulverston doctor whose family had lived in Drigg for many generations.

Between Drigg and the A595 road, and mainly along this road, is Holmrook, a small village of a few houses and shops. The post office is close to Drigg church, the pub is at the top of the hill on the main road. It is 'The Lutwidge Arms', named after the family at Holmrook Hall to the north.

Once an important Roman port, Ravenglass has just one cul-de-sac of a main street, ending at the seashore. It is an attractive village, and becoming very popular with amateur yachtsmen and boat enthusiasts. It is said to have been, in Roman times, the most important port in the north-west. Salt was shipped to it from Cheshire. There seems little doubt that it was Agricola's naval base, and that the Roman remains at Walls Castle were once a fortress guarding it. Since then the harbour has silted up quite badly. There is also a theory that Ravenglass may be linked through King Eveling to the Arthurian legends. This King and his court are mentioned by Camden in Elizabethan days after his visit to Cumberland in 1599. King John granted a charter permitting a market and annual fair, both now obsolete. At the fair, in early August, horse racing was part of the celebrations, until about 1813. This probably took place on the stretch of sands mentioned at Drigg, and now a nature reserve, with the largest black-headed gull colony in Britain. More than 12,000 pairs are known to nest there.

The village has a post office and 'The Pennington Arms Hotel'. The Pennington family have been connected with Ravenglass and Muncaster Castle, to the east, for some seven centuries. H. de Vere Stacpoole, the author and doctor whom we encountered earlier at Langwathby also spent a good deal of his time as a locum in Ravenglass. The principal attraction for visitors today is the miniature steam railway, the Ravenglass and Eskdale Railway, known locally and affectionately as 'La'al Ratty'. This is a working fifteen-inch gauge railway, with scheduled services and the right to carry Her Majesty's Mail and to issue stamps. It travels a seven-mile course through some truly magnificent scenery. It started life as a three-foot gauge railway in 1875, for the transportation of iron ore. Passengers were first carried in 1876. The line was closed to passengers in 1908, and then closed completely in 1912. It was changed to a fifteen-inch gauge and re-opened in 1916, but was again closed to passengers between 1939 and 1946, during the war. It was put up for sale in 1958. A Preservation Society was formed the following year and the line was saved, the present company taking over in 1961.

Bootle is a very pleasant small village astride the A595, which, in fact, cuts its graveyard in two. The right of the inhabitants to hold a market was granted by a charter of Edward III in 1348 and renewed by Queen Elizabeth in 1567. The ancient market cross has been replaced by the present one, standing next to the churchyard and put there for Queen Victoria's Diamond Jubilee in 1897. Dominating the skyline above the village is the mass of Black Combe (1,970 ft.), whose bracken-covered sides are breathtakingly lovely in autumn. Two poets have written about it, Wordsworth and the modern, Millom-born, Norman Nicholson. It is claimed that the view from its summit is the most extensive from any point in Britain, and that fourteen counties in England and Scotland can be seen, together with Snowdon, the Isle of Man, and the Mountains of Mourne. In the village, the post office is a good-sized store. An Independent chapel dated 1780 is now the Congregational church. The house next door is also dated 1780. The pub is 'The King's Head Hotel'. The school, still in use, carries a plaque dated 1830 with texts carved on it from Ecclesiastes and Proverbs including, 'Train up a child in the way he should go, and when he is old he will not depart from it'. The church dedicated to St. Michael is ancient, but had extensive repairs in 1837 and again in 1891. It is a cruciform church with a pinnacled tower. In the churchyard is a sundial perched high on stone steps. The font has initials in shields and other carvings of the words '*In nomine Patris, Filii, et Spiritus Sancti*'. The old oil lamps have been wired for electric lighting. There is a brass of Sir Hugh Askew who died in 1562; he was knighted by Edward VI at the battle of Pinkie (Musselburgh). The name Bootle means 'the dwelling'. A good deal of ugly recent development is tucked away behind the village and towards the railway station, one and a quarter miles away. At the station is a post office and 'The Railway Hotel'.

The village of Whitbeck, 'white stream', is nothing more than a few scattered farms and a church at the foot of Black Combe. According to local belief neither fish nor ducks will live in the stream, yet cattle drink it without ill-effect. The church, dedicated to St. Mary, has a bell-cote with two bells, surmounted by a stone cross. It is a plain, very simple church restored in 1883. The only stained glass is a small square, showing the head of Christ wearing the crown of thorns, in the otherwise clear east window. Near the font is a very sadly worn and mutilated six-foot effigy of a woman wearing a wimple and veil and with her feet resting on a dog. It is said to represent the Lady of Annaside.

Another small village not far away, and with a church similarly dedicated to St. Mary and bearing a similar bell-cote with stone cross, is Whicham. The village consists mainly of recent bungalows and houses. The school near the church was founded in 1540 as the Whicham and Millom Grammar School. It was re-built in 1862. The church is ancient but was restored in 1858 and again in 1901. It is large and rectangular, almost barn-like, inside, but attractive. A pleasing east window shows scenes from the life of Christ. Tablets to those who died in both World Wars are in the church, and beside them is displayed the Victoria Cross won by a man born in the parish and awarded the decoration for most conspicuous gallantry in 1917. This is the only instance I know of a church displaying this high decoration.

Just off the Millom road is Silecroft, the 'croft where sallows grow'. Its 'Miners Arms' is a first class inn behind a somewhat unprepossessing exterior. There is a post office-store, a village hall, and a railway station. A house nearby is dated 1798. Beyond the village and close to the excellent beach is a spacious caravan site and golf course. Farther along the Millom road is Kirksanton, a cluster of houses and farms. 'The King William IV Hotel' stands beside the road.

Haverigg, which grew to be almost a small town, is now facing a decline. There is much derelict property at its eastern end. It has one long main street with recent housing developments off it. Its post office is also a shop, and there are several other stores. On the outskirts is one of H.M. Prisons. The church was built in 1891 as a chapel-of-ease to St. George's church, Millom. It is dedicated to St. Luke. An upturned bell serves as a flower-pot just inside the churchyard gate. A memorial for the 1914–18 war stands in the churchyard. It is a very simple church. The east window is the only one with stained glass, and this has a rather luminescent appearance. The Primitive Methodist chapel dated 1870 is now used as the Over 60s Club. The Chapel of Bible Christians, 1873, with Sunday School attached (1881), is the present Methodist church. There is a Working Men's Club and two pubs, 'The Harbour Hotel' and 'The Rising Sun'. Beside the dunes is a caravan site and a children's playground. From there, Barrow-in-Furness can be seen across the Duddon Sands. At low water something like 13,000 acres of sands are bare. The river Duddon comes down from the Wrynose Pass, following a course of about twenty-five miles to where it joins the Irish Sea at Haverigg. Norman Nicholson, speaking of Wordsworth's romanticized view, writes:

> But you and I know better, Duddon.
> For I, who've lived for nearly thirty years
> Upon your shore, have seen the slagbanks slant
> Like screes into the sand, and watched the tide
> Purple with ore back up the muddy gullies,
> And wiped the sinter dust from the farmyard damsons.

Listed as a village, and just off the A5093, is The Green. It is a scattering of houses and farms with the village green as their focal point. Around the green are the post office-store, 'The Punch Bowl Inn', and the village hall, 1968, with adjacent reading room, 1948.

8

The Northern Lake District

MOST of the villages between Maryport and Penrith lie in the western, flatter part of the area—along both sides of the A595 and north of Bassenthwaite Lake. A few skirt the north Lakeland fells, and there are a few more where the flatter land begins again towards Penrith.

Mealsgate is a scattered village, taking in the part called Fletchertown. There is a post office in Mealsgate on the main A595 road where the signpost to Boltongate says one and a half miles. (The one at Boltongate says 'Mealsgate 2 miles'!). There is also a post office at Fletchertown, with the shops, a social club and the school. The 1894 Wesleyan chapel is now the Methodist church. The former 'Appletree Inn' at Mealsgate is now derelict. George Moore (1806–76), who became a very wealthy merchant in London, was born at Mealsgate. He was a great philanthropist and was offered many honours, most of which he declined. He used to tell of walking into Carlisle as a boy to see a public hanging and then walking back to Mealsgate in the evening. The house he had built in the village in 1861, 'Whitehall', is still lived in, but is in a state of disrepair. There is a tablet to commemorate him in Carlisle Cathedral. He died as the result of a street accident and was buried in the old church at Mealsgate. This church, of All Hallows, was built in 1587 and was restored by Moore in 1862. Only the Norman chancel of it remains today, a few hundred yards from 'Whitehall'. It can be reached by going down a rough track leading off a lay-by south-west of the post office, and then along a narrow footpath to where the chancel is hidden in a clump of trees. The path and the old churchyard are overgrown, but the ruins are worth a visit to see the memorial tablets and sculptures to George Moore and members of his family. He who did so much good during his lifetime is so shockingly neglected in death. The new church of All Hallows is through Fletchertown, on the Aspatria road; it was built in 1896–9. Pevsner calls it 'a satisfying, honest interior'. It is a long, plain church with bench seats. In it is a plaque given by the city of Paris in 1962 in recognition of the help given to that city by George Moore in 1870.[1] The French Government had conferred on Moore the Cross of the Legion of Honour.

Not far away is the quite large village of Blennerhasset, its houses radiating from its village green. Ekwall interprets the name as meaning 'hill-farm hay-shieling'. The war memorial is on the green. Above a shop doorway facing it is the claim that the shop was founded by a 'gentleman philanthropist', the fourth son of a baronet. On the other side of the green is Peare Tree House, dated 1686. There is a village hall, and a small, corrugated-iron church and Sunday School—a chapel-of-ease to Torpenhow. The Independent chapel of 1828 still stands, but is no longer in use. Next to it is a row of dilapidated seventeenth-century cottages. The former reading room and library was built in 1890 by Sir Wilfrid Lawson, the father of the 'gentleman philanthropist' who founded the shop, and adjoins it. 'The Grey Goat' inn is just outside the village, on the other side of the river Ellen. An early experiment in co-operative farming was tried in the village from 1862–72.

Plumbland, 'plum tree grove', is for the most part just one long main street. The former Congregational chapel, still bearing its plaque 'God is love, 1847', is now the Plumbland Evangelical chapel. The school, with a church-like tower, was founded in 1759 but not built until 1799. The stream skirting the village on the east, the Popple, was popularly said to have run blood on the day King Charles I was beheaded. This was a belief shared by several other villages about their streams. 'The Horse and Jockey Inn' and 'The Inglewood' are in Parsonby on the Aspatria road. Plumbland church is also in Parsonby—hence the name—and this gave rise to a couplet:

[1] Paris was besieged by the Germans, during the Franco-Prussian War, from September 1870 to January 1871.

The greatest wonder ever was seen
Is Plumbland church on Parsonby green.

The church is dedicated to St. Cuthbert, and one window shows the Saint carrying the head of St. Oswald. It was built in 1870–1 and is entered through what looks like a cupboard in the porch. It is far too big for present needs. The chancel arch is Norman, but was made higher when the church was re-built. The glass in the east window is to members of the Dykes family who lived for many generations at Ward Hall. One of the family, Thomas Dykes, was an ardent Royalist. After the battle of Marston Moor he was hunted by Cromwell's soldiers, and hid for a time in a mulberry tree, being fed by his wife and daughter who brought food from the Hall. He was later captured and died in Cockermouth Castle. The mulberry tree is still there. Fragments of an Anglo-Danish hogback tombstone are in the churchyard under a large yew. The square building in the adjacent field is said to be a fourteenth-century manorial pigeon-house.

A very long village with quite a number of roads leading into it is Gilcrux, largely a farming community. Its pub is 'The Masons Arms'. The school was re-built in 1864 and enlarged in 1898. The 1875 Wesleyan chapel is said to be on the very spot where John Wesley stood and preached. The item of real note, however, is the old, grey stone church with its single bell-cote. It is dedicated to St. Mary and dates back to the fourteenth century, with earlier Norman work still visible. It was restored in 1878. It is a delightful little church, especially to an observer standing at the west end and looking through the narrow chancel arch towards the east window. This window contains the only (1937) stained glass. There is a large, irregular sort of hagioscope in the chancel arch. An old font inside the door is painted white. The Royal Arms are of George II. The small, deep-set windows show the thickness of the walls. The reredos is a copy in glass of Leonardo's *Last Supper*, installed in 1865 and now adapted so that it can be illuminated from behind. Set at an angle above the porch is an 1836 sundial. Gilcrux was the birthplace of Joseph Jackson (died 1789), the philosopher and scientist who tried to disprove Newton's theory.

He died while on his way home from Spain where he had gone to open a colliery, in Andalusia.

Belying the meaning of its name, 'enclosure for deer', modern Dearham is a grim and depressing village set on the Cumberland coalfield. It possesses a large school, a post office, a Methodist church, and three pubs—'The Old Ship Inn', 'The Queen's Head', and 'The Globe Inn'. The Primitive Methodist chapel, 1836, is disused. The village's great glory lies in the stones inside its church of St. Mungo (Kentigern). This is a Norman church restored and enlarged in 1882. The tower was added as a place of refuge during the Border wars. There are old tombstones, etc., built into the walls of the porch and on the north side of the church, and the solid Norman font is interestingly carved. Three other pieces, however, are the most memorable, all dating from about A.D. 900. One is the Adam Stone, representing the fall and restoration of man and showing Adam and Eve with God and the serpent; the second is the Kenneth Cross, giving the legend of the sixth-century hermit brought up by seagulls; and the third is the magnificent wheel-head cross, five feet four inches high, carved with the Yggdrasil, great world ash tree of Scandinavian mythology adopted into early Christianity as the Tree of Life. Until fairly recently the cross stood outside in the churchyard. A tablet in the porch is in memory of a boy of nine and a half who was drowned in 1836. The 1891 Sunday school and hall is adjacent to the church. Dearham was the birthplace of John White (1866–1933), who spent most of his life in Southern Rhodesia, and founded a college there. He translated the New Testament into the tribal languages.

Tallentire, 'end of the land', is a village of grey houses and farms set at varying angles. There is some new building in progress. The village has its school (1863), post office, and pub—'The Bush Inn'. The 1876 Congregational chapel is no longer in use but still has the words 'Worship the Lord in the beauty of holiness' above its door.

The village of Bridekirk is unremarkable, being mainly old farms and recent houses. The name means 'the church of St. Bride, or Bridget', the fifth-century Irish saint. The present church which bears her name was built in 1870 incorporating part of the old church, some remains of which are still in the churchyard. Ancient tombstones stand round the walls of the cruciform church, which has a Norman arch in its porch. Inside it has an unusual reredos of fleur-de-lys patterned tiles, set into red terra cotta interlaced arches, the whole in the shape of an apse. There is an interesting recent Good Samaritan window. The church's outstanding feature is its twelfth-century font, one of the finest pieces of Norman sculpture in the country. A Runic inscription is interpreted as a statement that 'Rikarth' or Richard made the font, and he is depicted on one side working away with his chisel and mallet. The font alone is ample repayment for a visit. Two men who achieved considerable fame were born in the nearby vicarage. Sir Joseph Williamson (1633–1701) became the Secretary of State in 1674. A few years later he was shut up in the Tower of London by order of Parliament, but was released by the King a few hours later. He was President of the Royal Society, and is buried in Westminster Abbey. Thomas Tickell (1686–1740) was a poet and statesman. He was a friend of Joseph Addison, and is remembered chiefly for his poem, highly praised by Dr. Johnson, Macaulay and others, lamenting the death of his friend:

> Can I forget the dismal night that gave
> My soul's best part for ever to the grave?

On the eastern side of the A595 is Blindcrake, 'top rock'. It is a village of grey houses and farms, some dating from 1719, 1728 and 1729. From it there are lovely views of the woods of the National Park to the south-east. The Methodist chapel of 1894 was converted out of dwelling-houses, as was the reading room, opened in 1877. The latter is used as the village hall and also for occasional Anglican services. The village pump has disappeared, but in the wall beside the road where it stood a tablet bears the inscription—'As birds drink, and straight lift up their head, So must man, sip and think, Of better drink, He may attain to, after he is dead'. Franklin Engelman of the B.B.C. 'Down your way' programme held one of his interviews in the kitchen bar of 'The Ghyll Yeat Inn'.

The tiny village of Sunderland, as its name indicates ('separate land'), is quite on its own, well removed from other places. It has one house dated 1740, and boasts a telephone kiosk and a post box. Bothel, where the Keswick road joins the A595, has fine views across the Solway to Criffel (1,866 ft.) and south Scotland. In former times a day and night watch was kept over the Solway for hostile ships approaching the coast, and an alarm beacon was kept ready for lighting. There is a post office-general store. The 1890 Methodist church has been restored. This is another village where, by tradition, the beck ran red on the day of the martyrdom of Charles I. The village has three pubs—'The Loft House Hotel' with large antlers above its door, 'The Queen's Head Inn', and 'The Greyhound Inn'. The name stands for 'the dwelling'.

Torpenhow, 'the top or breast of the hill', has a Country Towns Mission Hall, deserted and neglected, with a sundial on its wall bearing the legend 'As thy day so shall thy strength be'. It was formerly used for religious services by 'members of the Dissenting body'. The Memorial School, 1855, is no longer used for that purpose but as a field centre. There is a post office-store, 'The Sun Inn', an ex-army hut used as the village hall, and a house dated 1690. The church, dedicated to St. Michael, is one of the few unspoilt twelfth-century churches. The exterior was restored in 1913. Some Roman stones are incorporated into the building. Additional building work took place in 1160, 1260 and during a thorough restoration in 1882. The entrance door and the chancel arch are Norman. On one side of the chancel arch are carved odd faces, including that of a hippopotamus, and on the other side a group of little men linking arms and legs. The nave ceiling strikes an unusual note. It probably came from a London Livery Company's hall and is painted with cupids and garlands. It was given to the church in 1689 by Thomas Addison, brother of the more famous Joseph Addison. The churchyard commands beautiful views to the north.

Along the Caldbeck road from Mealsgate is Boltongate, a small village on a hill. Its post office is at the rectory. Nearby is 'The White Swan Inn'. There is a cottage dated 1687. From the south side of the church there is a beautiful view of Skiddaw. In the churchyard is the memorial to the men who died in the 1914–18 war. A tablet to the six who gave their lives between 1939 and 1945 is beside the churchyard gate. The Bell Church Institute,

1883, is next to the church. The church looks unusual from the outside. Inside it has pointed tunnel-vaulting, and colourful windows in the west end. Most unusual, however, are the varied accounts of its building. It is dedicated to All Saints, and is of cruciform plan. According to one authority it was built by the Earl of Westmorland, mentioned in Shakespeare's *Henry V* as one of the 'band of brothers' before the Battle of Agincourt. Local folklore has for a long time attributed the building to the Scottish wizard, Michael Scott, who died about 1291. He was a learned man believed to be in league with the forces of evil, and the church is reputed to have been finished in one night by his 'imps'. Supernaturally aided or not, Bishop Goodwin in the second half of last century said of the church that 'mathematically it ought to have fallen down, because the weight of the massive stone roof should have forced the walls out'. It is also held that the church was erected by workmen imported from France. Were they, perhaps —speaking a foreign language, and maybe working faster than the British workman was wont to do—the origin of the 'imps' legend? Whatever the truth the church is certainly ancient.

Keats wrote about 'rustic festivities' at the inn at Ireby in 1818. Today it is a village which has diminished in importance because the market is no longer held there. The market charter was granted in 1237, and the market attracted so much trade at one time that Cockermouth was in danger of being ruined by it. The Market Cross still stands. Not far away is 'The Black Lion Inn', with 'The Sun Inn' towards the church. The old Moot Hall[1] is now converted into houses. There is a post office-store as well as another store. The village hall is dated 1908. There is a very active Women's Institute, with its own headquarters since 1952. A house in the village is dated 1684. The church of St. James was built in 1845–6, largely from stones taken from the old church when its nave was pulled down in 1845. The west wall shows the old stone; the other walls are plastered. It is a wide oblong church, obviously well cared for, but nevertheless cold looking. The seating, altar and pulpit came from St. John's church, Uldale, when it was being demolished in 1961. The font is twelfth-century workmanship and came from the old church. The stained glass in the east window

[1] A town-hall or council chamber.

is modern, about 1950. There are old stones in the porch. Ireby old church, of which only the chancel remains, stands in a field about a mile west of the village on the Torpenhow road. It is late Norman, about 1170, and has an interesting 1626 monument to George Crage in the south wall. This chancel is now in the care of the National Redundant Churches Fund. The name Ireby stands for 'the settlement of the Irish'.

Uldale, 'wolves valley', is set halfway up the Uldale Fells above the river Ellen, with the patchwork fields of the lower land to the north. It is a small village built around the crossroads at its village green. The inn is 'The George and Dragon'. The ancient grammar school was replaced by the present school in 1895. It carries a tablet erected by the governors of the grammar school. There is not much new building. In 1868 a new church of St. John was built to replace the old church; this became unsafe about 1954 and was finally demolished in 1963. Meanwhile worship had been resumed in the low, whitewashed church of St. James, along the Ireby road. It has a 1915 lych-gate, and a twin bell-cote. Inside, it is a pleasant though rather bleak little church. There is a tablet to a former teacher at the grammar school who emigrated to North Carolina in 1763 and made his fortune. Another tells of gifts to the poor of the parish by a native who died at Henley-on-Thames in 1773. The doors at the west end came from St. Mary's church, Carlisle, when it was demolished in 1955. John Peel's wife, Mary White, was an Uldale woman. Her mother forbade the banns, so the young couple fled to Gretna Green.

A little bridge over a laughing stream leads to the compact grey little village of Bassenthwaite, at the foot of mighty Skiddaw (3,053 ft.). Bassenthwaite Hall beside the stream is now a farm. A plaque above the door of a small house near 'The Sun Inn' reads —'This house done by John Grave 1736'. The post office is a private house beside the large village green. The Methodist chapel adjoins the 1874 reading room which appears to be a builder's store. Bassenthwaite possesses two churches. That of St. John the Evangelist, built in 1878, is beside the main road to Keswick, half a mile south of the village. It is a grey, not very attractive church, with a long, thin, ugly spire. There is 1961 stained glass in the south wall, and inferior 1900 glass in the apse of the east

The giant yew-tree at Lorton of which Wordsworth wrote: 'There is a yew-tree, pride of Lorton Vale, which to this day stands single in the midst of its own darkness. . . .'

Buttermere church. The village lies below, with beyond it the waterfalls of Sour Milk Gill

(*left*) The grave, at Finsthwaite church, of Prince Charles Edward Stuart's natural daughter Clementina
(*right*) This cross of local stone marks the grave of John Ruskin, who was buried in Coniston churchyard

Lindale village, with the iron obelisk which is a memorial to John Wilkinson, the great iron master

end. The nave presents a cold, bare appearance, particularly when viewed from the chancel. The other, older church is close beside the lake, two miles to the south. It is the church of St. Bega, that well repaid for me a walk across two large fields. For it was sitting at the water's edge, near this church, that Tennyson composed the beautiful lines in his *Morte d'Arthur* which tell of the sword Excalibur being cast into the water. It is a Norman church with a crooked chancel arch and interesting arches to the south aisle. Electric bulbs have been cunningly fitted into the old oil lamps. A small lead crucifix hanging above the 1874 pulpit is probably fourteenth-century. The Royal Arms of George II were installed at the time of Bonnie Prince Charlie's rebellion as a reminder where true loyalty should lie.

On the Cockermouth to Keswick road, straddling it, is Embleton. Most of the houses are to the north of the road, including 'The Wheatsheaf Inn' and the Methodist church. The latter was originally the Wesleyan chapel of 1863, re-built in 1904. Recently, however, worship has ceased in it, the Methodists having now joined with the Anglicans. On the south side of the road is the post office and 'Ye Blue Bell Inn'. South-west, and quite a distance from the village, is the church of St. Cuthbert. It was built in 1806 on the site of an older church, and was restored in 1886, when the present east window was inserted. Outside, it is somewhat unattractive with its stumpy tower. Inside it is plain, simple, but friendly. The east window is slightly out of balance. The mosaic reredos is not at all attractive. One can only assume that the village has developed along the developing main road, leaving the church to become more and more solitary.

Crosthwaite, 'the clearing by a cross', although now a residential suburb of Keswick, is of greater antiquity. In the middle of the sixth century, St. Kentigern set up a cross and preached on what is now the spot where Crosthwaite church stands dedicated to him. Major restoration work was carried out on the church in 1844–5. It is a most notable church with far too many features to be enumerated in the space available here. Of particular interest are the fourteenth-century font; the east window by Charles E. Kempe (1837–1907); the Ratcliffe brasses; the colours of the Skiddaw Greys; and the white marble figure of Robert

Southey (1774–1843), the Poet Laureate, by the sculptor John G. Lough (1798–1876), with an epitaph by Wordsworth. Southey's grave in the churchyard was restored in 1961 by the generosity of the Brazilian Government. Near it is an indicator, pointing to and identifying the various mountains which can be seen. Also buried in the churchyard is Elizabeth Lynn Linton (1822–98), the novelist and writer on the Lake District—she was the first woman newspaper writer to draw a fixed salary. Canon H. D. Rawnsley, one of the founders of the National Trust, was vicar of Crosthwaite for thirty-four years, and he, too, is buried there. A memorial to him stands at Friars Crag beside Derwentwater. A vault was uncovered in the church in 1972 where Edward Stephenson was buried. He was born at Keswick in 1691 and was appointed Governor of Bengal in 1728, but his Governorship lasted for only thirty-five hours. The school adjoining the churchyard is also of very old foundation. In the village is a recently enlarged Roman Catholic church and the pub, 'The Pheasant Inn'.

Set back from the A591 road and tucked in at the very foot of Skiddaw (3,053 ft.) is an attractive cluster of houses and farms, Applethwaite, 'the clearing where apples grow'. Quite close is Underskiddaw church room and beside it the war memorial to both wars.

Just to the north of the Keswick to Penrith road is Threlkeld, 'the spring of the thralls'. It lies below Blencathra (2,847 ft.), from which both the local hunt and the local hospital get their names. It is quite a large village with much recent and new development. Some of the people find employment locally at the hospital or at the granite quarry. Sheep dog trials are held in the summer. There are one or two small stores. The village hall, 'The Public Room', was built in 1901; the school in 1849, enlarged in 1879. Every child on leaving the school is given a copy of the New Testament. The 1885 mission room is now closed. The church, dedicated to St. Mary, was built in 1777, to replace a thatched church which almost certainly replaced an even earlier one. One of the subscribers to the new church was Wordsworth's early patron, Raisley Calvert. It is a pleasant, clean, though unremarkable, church which was restored in 1910–11, when most of the present woodwork was installed, as was the font of Threlkeld granite. The ugly bell tower and the two bells were incorporated from the old church. The early marriage register, which begins in 1573, speaks of a rather unusual custom—'Formal contracts of marriage are herein recorded; and sureties entered for the payment of five shillings to the poor by the party that draws back'. It is still common during a wedding service for young people to tie the two churchyard gates securely together. 'The Horse and Farrier Inn' is dated 1688. There is also 'The Salutation Inn'.

Where the river Glenderamackin tumbles down from Souther Fell to meet the obstruction of Raven Crags and turn back southwards again, is the tiny, enchanting village of Mungrisdale. It has a village hall, and 'The Mill Inn'. It has also the tiny whitewashed church of St. Kentigern, with its single bell-cote and bell, and thick moss making its roof a bright green. A church has stood on this spot since about A.D. 552. The present one was re-built in 1756. Its cobbled porch leads into the barn-shaped church. The three-decker pulpit has the date 1679. There is a tablet to Raisley Calvert (also mentioned at Threlkeld) whose son, also Raisley, was nursed by Wordsworth while he was dying of consumption, and left the poet £900. It was on Souther Fell in 1743 that quite a number of people witnessed, and attested on oath before a magistrate that they had seen, spectral horsemen and troops passing over the mountain side and visible for some two hours. My own earliest contact with the village was many years ago, to examine the ravens' nests with that skilful taxidermist Ernest Blezard, who reproduced an exact replica of a nest for the Bird Room in Carlisle City Museum. Ekwall gives the meaning of 'grisdale' as 'pigs valley' (as in the village of Grizedale)—'Mun' was added several centuries later and could stand for Mungo (Kentigern).

At one side of Greystoke green are older grey stone houses which contrast with the modern ones on the housing estate on the other side. On the green itself is the tall, graceful and ancient cross. A road leads under an archway to the grounds of Greystoke Castle and the stables of Sir Gordon Richards, the one-time champion jockey. Opposite the green is the sixteenth-century inn, 'The Boot and Shoe'. There is a village hall, a post office-shop, and a school with iron-studded doors, dated 1838. Along the lane leading to the church, protected by an iron grille, is the medieval sanctuary stone. The large, collegiate, slightly cathedral-like church is dedicated to St. Andrew. It claims to have the most extensive examples of the perpendicular style in England. The oak stalls in the chancel have carved misericord seats, though nothing like so fine as those in Carlisle Cathedral. The lovely east window was restored in 1848 and contains the church's medieval glass. One window shows St. Andrew trampling on a red, prostrate devil. This is one of the only two windows in England showing the red devil. An interesting brass is in memory of Henry Askew who was killed in France in 1914 and buried by the Germans with a cross bearing the words 'Here lies a brave British officer'. Two alabaster effigies of knights are fourteenth and fifteenth century. Above them, hanging from the west wall, is a modern 'crucifixion' by Josephina de Vasconcellos, the wife of Delmar Banner. There is a 1710 cube-shaped sundial in the churchyard. The ancient collegiate character of the church was restored in 1958, by the formation of a scheme for assisting young men who wish to enter the ministry.

9

The Central Lake District

THIS chapter includes the scattered villages in the area which covers Haweswater, Ullswater, Grasmere, Thirlmere, Derwentwater, Crummock Water, Buttermere, Loweswater, Ennerdale Water and Wastwater. It is lovely, wild country, which was almost unknown to people living in the rest of England until the French Revolution stopped Englishmen doing the Grand Tour of Europe and forced them to get to know more about their own country. It still contains more hamlets than villages. To most people this is *the* Lake District and they flock to it in the summer months in such numbers that they virtually destroy the qualities they have gone there to find. For sheer beauty, as well as for pleasanter visting, the spring and autumn are the best times, although nature can be in her most awesome glory in the bleak mid-winter. One must admit that tourism, and its own grandeur, has brought hitherto unaccustomed wealth to the Lake District towns and villages—but oh, how much besides!

Only a short step west of the motorway is Yanwath—'flat wood'. It is only a small village straggling down a cul-de-sac alongside the main railway line. The pub, 'The Gate Inn', is on the Pooley Bridge, B5320, road. It has mounting-steps outside it. At the opposite end of the cul-de-sac is Yanwath Hall, probably the finest manorial hall in the country. The large, square pele-tower built by John de Sutton in 1322 is the most dominating feature. The Hall passed to the Lowthers in 1671 and still forms part of the Lowther estate. It is now a farmhouse. The Quaker Thomas Wilkinson (1751–1836) was born at Yanwath. He once walked (in 1791) from there via Stainmoor to London in eight days to attend a Quaker meeting. He became a friend of Wordsworth, and wrote on first meeting the poet—"He is very sober, and very amiable, and writes in what he conceives to be the language of Nature in opposition to the finery of our present poetry".

A mile or so farther along the B5320 is the small grey village of Tirril. It has new residential building behind it but still preserves the village appearance. There is a Wesleyan chapel dated 1879. On the village green is what appears to be the base of a cross. The post office-store is on one side of the green, the 1914 reading room and library on the opposite side. Nearby is a barn dated 1767, and behind it a house dated 1735. Another has above the door the date, 1765, and the words 'To Know Thyself is a Proof of Wisdom'. 'The Queen's Head' inn is dated 1719, a house close to it, 1712. At the far end of the village is 'The Old Meeting House', dated 1733 and now a private house. It was, of course, originally the Quaker Meeting House and later became the reading room before the present one was built. In front of the house is an enclosure which was the Friends' burial ground and contained, earlier this century, the grave of the young man called Charles Gough who was killed on Helvellyn in 1805. His body was not found for three months, and had been guarded all that time by his faithful dog. Scott and Wordsworth both used the story. There are now no gravestones in the cemetery. Sockbridge is now more or less joined to Tirril by recent housing development. Wordsworth's grandfather lived there; he was the first of the family to settle in Westmorland.

Askham, 'the place of ash trees', is an ancient village with quite a number of recent houses and a large village green split in two by the Haweswater road. The new houses do not spoil the look of the old village, with its unusually large number of dated, old houses—1650, 1674, 1683, 1708, 1712, 1716, 1724 and 1763. 'The Queen's Head' is a fascinating pub dated 1682. Near it is the post office-shop, the village hall and the swimming pool which was (in 1972) in process of construction. Another pub, 'The Punch Bowl', lies down the hill towards the church. The shell of Lowther Castle can be seen amongst the trees across the river. The church, of St. Peter, was built on the site of an older one by Robert Smirke in 1832. He had built Lowther Castle twenty to twenty-five years earlier. The church is set amongst trees away from the village and beside the river Lowther. It is a pleasant simple church with no stained glass. Its lighting was a thank-offering for the victory of the Allies in 1945. There are tablets to the dead of both World Wars in the church, and a gallery at the west end. The most interesting feature is the pre-sixteenth-century south transept, which was for long the burial chapel of the Sandfords who lived at Askham Hall from 1375 to 1680. This part of the church was dedicated as a baptistry in 1950, and contains the 1661 font. The cost of the work was met by a Pennsylvania (United States) man who had in his youth been a gardener at Askham, and who loved his native village.

On the opposite side of the river is Lowther, 'foaming river', and at the top of the hill, barely half a mile from Askham church, stands Lowther church. It is virtually a monument to the Lowther family and the Earls of Lonsdale, for it is filled with their monumental brasses and other memorials in stone, mosaic, and carved wood, while in the churchyard is a great mausoleum, built in 1857, with the solitary seated figure of William, Earl of Lonsdale (1757–1844), in the upper part. It was to him that Wordsworth dedicated his poem *The Excursion.* An earlier Lowther, Sir James (1736–1802), had contributed to the introduction of the Reform Bill by his bribery of electors; particularly in the Carlisle elections of 1785 and 1786, when freemen were created wholesale until the campaign became known derisively as the 'mushroom election'. The most famous of the earls was the fifth (1857–1944), familiarly known as 'Lordy' or 'The Yellow Earl'. He was the patron of boxing, and the Lonsdale Belts, first fought for in 1909, originate from his interest. The Automobile Association's vehicles are a lasting tribute to him also. He was the Association's first president and permitted his yellow to be used on their vehicles, which are still recognized by that colour. The yellow flag of the Lonsdales hangs inside the church. It is dedicated to St. Michael and commands magnificent views over the river and the countryside. Askham Hall, the home of the present Earl of Lonsdale, can be seen from the churchyard. Not far from the church is Lowther New Town, an early effort at town planning. In about 1683–4 Sir John Lowther decided to replace the existing Lowther village, and the New Town lies just to the east of Lowther Castle. Another Lowther village lies half a mile further east, built between about 1765 and 1775. It is almost certainly the work of Robert Adam (1728–92). Lowther Castle was built on the site of Lowther Hall, where Mary Queen of Scots spent the night on her way from Carlisle Castle to her eventual execution. The present castle replaced an earlier one, and was the first commission of Robert Smirke, aged only twenty-five at the time. It was built between 1806 and 1811, and remained the home of the Lowther family until 1936. Regrettably only a façade remains today, the rest having been demolished in 1957.

Hackthorpe lies on the A6 road about one and a half miles south-east of Lowther Castle. Its pub is the Lowther Castle Hotel. It has a post office-shop. The entrance to the Lowther Wild Life Park, opened in May 1969, is on the outskirts.

The village of Helton, 'a place on the side of the hill', is just that. The houses, some looking quite old, are built along a street curving off the Askham–Bampton road in an arc on the hillside. One house is dated 1686. The pub is 'The Helton Inn', and there is a Wesleyan chapel dated 1867.

Approaching from the north, the first sight of the village of Bampton is of its roofs alone. There is a post office. The pub is 'St. Patrick's Well' and it is there that the Mardale Hunt meets since the submerging of Mardale village by the enlargement of Haweswater as a reservoir for Manchester in 1935. The church is at Bampton Grange where there is another pub, 'The Crown and Mitre', and houses dated 1705 and 1719. A cottage opposite the church boasts the name of 'Christian Cottage'. The Wesleyan chapel of 1877 is now the Methodist church. The Anglican church is one of only ten in the whole of England dedicated to St. Patrick; a church has existed on this site for at least eight hundred years. The present church was built in 1726–7. The chancel was restored in 1885. The font is believed to be twelfth century, the date 1662 having been carved on it later. The timber arcades in the church are most attractive. The east window is very dark. The reredos is of carved oak, and a fine piece of workmanship, with panels of inlaid holly. A portrait of the Reverend John Boustead (1754–1841) hangs in the church. He was master of Bampton Grammar

School and minister of Mardale Church. It was said of him that he had educated more students for the church than any other man in England. Two bishops were born in the parish. One was Edmund Gibson (1669–1748), who became Bishop of Lincoln and then of London. His portrait is in the church. The other bishop was Hugh Curwen (*c.* 1490–1568). He was cast in the mould of the notorious Vicar of Bray, for he was successively chaplain to Henry VIII, Roman Catholic Archbishop of Dublin under Queen Mary, and a Protestant after Elizabeth I came to the throne. There is also a painting of Mardale Church before it was inundated. The name Bampton stands for 'the place by the beam', probably a footbridge over the river Lowther.

The name of Shap has been known, and feared, by travellers of all sorts for many centuries. It is only two hundred years ago, in 1763 to be precise, that the first stage-coach was able to travel over Shap Fell. In later years many long-distance lorry-drivers and others have accepted hospitality in the village when their vehicles were stuck in snow or ice on the Fell. The motorway has changed all that, and now the long main street of Shap is much quieter. As one would expect, there are several shops, cafés and inns which came into being to cater for the traveller. One former coaching inn, 'The Greyhound Hotel', has an interesting old milestone beside its door. It also has over its door a white-painted model of a greyhound, and a queer, gilded depiction of one on a 1703 plaque on the wall. Other pubs are 'The Crown Inn', 'The Bull's Head', and 'The King's Arms Hotel'. The garage behind the last named was formerly the assembly rooms where Pot Fairs and Clothes Fairs used to be held. The village was granted a charter to hold a market in 1687. The present War Memorial Hall (so named after the 1914–18 war) was built in 1861 as The Market Hall. The Memorial Park, in memory of the men who died in the 1939–45 war, was opened in 1951 for the Festival of Britain. The old Market House stands halfway down the main street. The post office is small, and the school comparatively so, with its bell-cote and bell. There is a house dated 1691 and a cottage 1696. The church of St. Michael stands amongst trees above the main road. It was restored in 1898–9 but the older (some of them twelfth century) parts were retained. It is a plain stone church but rather nice, with a square tower under which the church is entered. The carved oak pulpit and altar are of 1899, as almost certainly is the Shap granite font. In the south chapel is a rather horrid painted plaster altar. Most interesting is a stone in the churchyard put there in memory of the 'workmen who lost their lives by accidents during the progress of the work on the Shap District of the Lancaster and Carlisle Railway'. The railway runs just behind the village. On the hillside above the village, the dead from Mardale churchyard were re-buried before the village was inundated by the extended reservoir of Haweswater in 1935. The remains of Shap Abbey to the west are all that is left of Westmorland's only abbey. South of the Abbey is the sixteenth-century Keld chapel, now owned by the National Trust. The very well-known Shap granite is quarried at works about three miles south of the village, and provides the major source of employment for the villagers. The name Shap means 'heap', and the village is shown as Heppe on old maps. This may stand for hip, the fruit of the dog-rose.

Stainton, the 'place on stony ground', near Penrith, is already a large village and is still developing. It is mostly recent, consisting of new houses and bungalows, although in the older part there are houses dated 1715, 1737, 1754 and 1787. There is a triangular village green. The Church of England school was opened in 1964. The pub is 'The Kings Arms' dated 1721, with mounting-steps outside it. Opposite is the village hall. The 1877 Methodist church is on the main Penrith–Keswick road, A66. Stainton had one of the oldest village cricket teams in Cumberland, but the club has just lost its pitch; after being played on for forty years, it is now required for housing development. A serviceman from the village was one of the coffin-bearers at the funeral of King Edward VIII (the Duke of Windsor) in 1972.

Farther along the A66 is the rather uninteresting village of scattered houses, some of them recent, making up Penruddock. The Presbyterian (now United Reformed) church, was re-built about 1789 on the site of an earlier one. The school was established in 1756 and re-built in 1872. It was formerly used for religious services, before the building of the drab little church of All Saints in 1902. The church has a bell-cote with single bell; it has no stained glass and no decoration at all beyond a memorial tablet to the dead of the 1914–18 war. The pub is 'The Norfolk Arms'.

Dacre, 'a trickling stream', beside Dacre Beck, is a charming village set in a hollow. The original parish school was built in 1749 and replaced in 1834. The post office is a private house; the pub is 'The Horse and Farrier'. The fourteenth-century pele-tower of the castle has walls seven feet thick. The glory of the village, however, is its lovely old church of St. Andrew. It is said to be built from the ruins of an ancient monastery mentioned by the Venerable Bede in his *Ecclesiastical History* (A.D. 731). In the churchyard four carved bears sit upright, one at each corner of the church. Pevsner thinks that these mark the four corners of the ancient churchyard. The Norman tower of the church was re-built in 1810. The new entrance-screen inside the church is in memory of a churchwarden who held the office from 1950–66. The communion-rail and the beams throughout the church look ancient. On a window-sill in the chancel is a piece of a cross-shaft dating from about A.D. 800 with a winged lion. Even more interesting is part of a tenth-century cross-shaft carved with Adam and Eve, with the tree and serpent and other animals, and with two men shown hand-in-hand. These two are said to represent King Athelstan of England and King Constantine of Scotland who met at Dacre in A.D. 926. Inside the sanctuary is a red sandstone effigy of a knight, fourteenth century, and is probably Ranulf, Lord Dacre. Nearby is the only example of Sir Francis Chantrey's work in the county. It is a kneeling female figure on a memorial tablet to Edward Hasell of Dalemain who died in 1825. On the south-west door is a large wooden lock given by Lady Anne Clifford and bearing the date 1671 and her initials A.P. (Anne of Pembroke). Very effective new lighting has been installed in the church recently.

The village of Pooley Bridge is on the Westmorland side of the bridge from which it gets part of its name. The other side of the bridge is in Cumberland. The bridge is built over the river Eamont where it emerges from lovely lake Ullswater. Pooley stands for the 'hill or mound by the pool', the hill being the thickly wooded semi-circular Dunmallet, west of the village and just inside the Cumberland boundary. It is obvious from the two hotels, 'The Sun Hotel' and 'The Crown Hotel', from the gift shops and the post office-shop, that Pooley Bridge caters for tourists. There is a good deal of recent residential building. The public shelter in the centre of the village has a fish weathervane. The village hall is the Memorial Hall, 1911. Next to it is St. Paul's church, built in 1868–9. It has no churchyard and is a small, plain church with a semi-circular communion rail, and uncomfortable-backed pews. The church is entered by way of a screen commemorating its centenary.

By the size of Barton church one would expect a large village instead of farms and houses scattered in ones and twos over a wide area. Kirkbarrow Hall, beside the Tirril road, is a Tudor house, now a farm, with a rather incongruous carved statuette above the door. The church is along a side road nearby which ends in the courtyard of Glebe Farmhouse. This house was at one time the vicarage. It has a plaque above the door with the date, 1637, and the words '*non mihi sed successoribus*'—not for me but for my successors. The Church of St. Michael is beautifully situated, with curving hills all round. It is part-Norman, and was built about 1150. The south aisle was added in 1250 because the church was found to be too small. The north aisle was then added fifty years later. The church was restored in 1904. It is a large, grey stone building with a square, squat twelfth-century tower, set centrally, and with five-foot-thick walls. The shield above the seventeenth-century porch is quartered with the arms of Lowther, Lancaster, Beauchamp and Hartson. There is a sundial over a small door in the south wall. On the north side is a very unusual church feature—a mounting-block close to what until not very many years ago were stables, with stalls for six horses—an indication of the distances some people had to come to church. The slates of this building are fixed with sheep's shank-bones instead of nails. The churchyard is entered under a 1920 lych-gate erected in honour of the men who gave their lives during the 1914–18 war. Inside, the church is a continuation of age and the unusual. The font is thirteenth-century. The Royal Arms are of George II. There is a large rectangular area in the centre, underneath the tower, and giving the impression of a tunnel. A 1673 brass beside the east window is to the wife of Lancelot Dawes, the man who built Glebe Farmhouse, and a verse inscribed on the plate claims that:

> Under this stone reader interred doth lye
> Beauty and virtues true epitomy;
> Atte her appearance the noone sun
> Blush'd and shrunk in cause quite undone.

From Pooley Bridge the road runs south-west close alongside the shore of Ullswater, a lake which many have thought to be amongst the most beautiful in the world. The Cumberland–Westmorland boundary is at the centre of the lake for most of its length. There is not much of Watermillock to see on the roadside—just a few houses and a filling station. The rest of the village is spread out from the lake-side at right-angles, up to the church about a mile distant. Knotts Hill Caravan Site is on the way. In the reign of Edward III (1327–77), there was a chapel beside the lake, but nothing seems to be known of its history. The present church, of All Saints, was opened in 1882. It is wonderfully situated on the site of an older church, out of sight of the lake, but to all appearances in a bowl of hills. Immediately above it, to the west, is Priest's Crag, said to have been well-wooded during the seventeenth century. However the noise of people hunting, nutting, and so on in the woods greatly aggravated the congregation, and the Bishop had the wood cut down. The church has a square tower with a stumpy spire. It is built of mauve slate and red sandstone. The Royal Arms are of George II. The bell commemorates the Diamond Jubilee (1897) of Queen Victoria. The altar is a plain table but its reredos is carved and painted with six winged cherubs. There is a memorial tablet to Sir Cecil A. S. Rice (1859–1918), who was H.M. Ambassador to the United States from 1913–18. It was he who wrote the words of the hymn, 'I vow to thee, my country'. There is also a tablet to a Canadian who fell at the Battle of the Somme in 1916.

Glenridding, 'beautiful clearing', is a village obviously catering for tourists. It has a pier jutting into Ullswater; a post office and a store; and the large 'Ullswater Hotel' on the main road. The main residential street is at right angles to the road and runs uphill towards the disused Greenside Mine. At its top end is 'The Travellers Rest' with an interesting inn sign. The 1890 Wesleyan chapel is now the Methodist church.

Beside the road between Glenridding and Patterdale, 'St. Patrick's Valley', is St. Patrick's Well. There is nothing to indicate what it is, and when I last saw it it was very much in need of cleaning out. It has been claimed that St. Patrick was shipwrecked on Duddon Sands on his way to Dublin in A.D. 540 and walked across to Patterdale and also to Bampton. Both places have churches dedicated to him. The Patterdale church was built in 1853. It has a curious clock tower on the north-east corner. It is a pleasant, though rather cold looking, church with a high ceiling. The chancel ceiling is painted with stars, perhaps in imitation of Carlisle Cathedral ceiling which was so decorated at about the same date. The solid font looks old. There is a white ensign from the Battle of Jutland, and on the south wall some fine examples of modern tapestry needlework. One says:

> Christ keep the mountain lands all the winter through,
> And bless the farms, and bless the school, and bless
> the fireside too.

No mention of people! Another, designed and worked by Ann Macbeth (1875–1948), is of Christ (I thought it was St. Patrick), showing him with sheep and lambs in a flower-strewn dales setting. The music beneath the scene is 'Jerusalem'; and Queen Mary, who was admiring the tapestry in a London exhibition, is said to have 'burst into song'. The village is dominated by Helvellyn (3,113 ft.) and St. Sunday Crag (2,756 ft.). Near the school, and opposite each other, are the 'White Lion Hotel' and 'The Patterdale Hotel'. The post office is also the general store. The youth hostel is at the Kirkstone end of the village.

Just before the climb up Kirkstone Pass, and along a narrow road to the east, is Hartsop. Its grey stone houses are typical of the fell-side villages. The road has no continuation beyond the village. Due south, the conical hill of Hartsop Dod (2,018 ft.) looks down.

At the south end of Derwentwater is a bridge much painted by artists. It leads to the tiny, picturesque village of Grange-in-

Borrowdale. It is a place often mentioned in the *Herries* stories by Sir Hugh Walpole (1884–1941). It is completely surrounded by hills, and is a very popular resort in the summer when its inadequate provision for car parking becomes apparent, and when the area beside the river Derwent looks like a lido. There is a post office-store. The Wesleyan chapel, originally built in 1859 and re-built in 1894, is now the Methodist church. The Anglican church, dedicated to the Holy Trinity, is of grey slate. It is a simple, pleasant and cared-for church. The unusual ceiling is barrel shaped, with six rows of what look like saw teeth pointing downwards. There is no stained glass. The porch is a separate little building. Outside the church, and matching it in colour, is the war memorial cross. The church was built in 1860 by Miss M. Heathcote, and the 1894 school is erected in her memory. Peace How, west of the village, was given by Canon Rawnsley in 1917 as a war memorial to the men of Keswick. It is now National Trust property. Borrowdale formerly belonged to Furness Abbey and at that time there were a few monks at Grange.

Borrowdale church is off the road beyond Rosthwaite. It is a small, plain structure re-built in 1825 and restored in 1873. Inside, it is of the school-room type. There are panels to the fallen of both World Wars, and also a panel to the great-grandson of William Wilberforce, the anti-slavery campaigner. The churchyard contains quite a number of tombstones with verses on them. Rosthwaite itself is rather similar to Grange, though not so picturesque. Most of it, and the large village hall, lies off the main road. There is a post office-store. Visitors are catered for at 'The Royal Oak Hotel' and 'The Scafell Hotel', while one guest house advertises itself as 'The Home of Rogue Herries'. Until the middle of the eighteenth century a cart was unknown in Borrowdale, all loads being transported on horseback. A native of the dale is sometimes called a 'Borrowdale Gowk' from the story of simple Borrowdale folk who built a wall in an attempt to keep in the gowk, or cuckoo, and so ensure perpetual spring!

Portinscale, according to Ekwall, has the rather unexpected meaning of 'the prostitute's hut'. It is now mainly a high-class residential village. There is a mission room, a post office-shop, 'The Farmers Arms Inn', and several large hotels, including the

'Tower Hotel' which at the beginning of this century was a college for young gentlemen.

Braithwaite, the 'broad clearing', is a small village with a good deal of recent residential development, just south of the Keswick–Cockermouth road. The Cumberland Pencil Company started in the village about 1868 but was burned down in 1898, and moved to Keswick. There are two pubs, 'The Royal Oak' and 'The Coledale Inn'. The post office is a private house. The school, originally built in 1842, was restored and extended in 1967. Next to it is the church, built in 1900, on the site of the former mission room, and dedicated to St. Herbert, the local saint who was a hermit on an island in Derwentwater and a close friend of St. Cuthbert. The only stained glass in the church is the pleasant east window illustrating the theme 'suffer little children to come unto me'. The recent motel was built against the wishes of many of the villagers, and one of them planted six cards inside the brickwork of the construction stating this fact.

Braithwaite was formerly linked with Thornthwaite as one community but both have now grown, with recent residential development, and each has its own post office and church. They do, however, share a Victory Memorial Hall built in 1927 between them. The houses of Thornthwaite are on the hillside at one side of the road. The church stands alone on the opposite side. It is dedicated to St. Mary, and is a plain, cruciform structure recently restored. It has a bell-tower and single bell. The stained glass is all of the uninteresting 1860 to 1870 period. The seventeenth-century 'Swan Hotel' was formerly 'The Swan with Two Necks'.

The Vale of Lorton runs, like the river Cocker, north-westwards from Crummock Water to Cockermouth. It is a lovely, fertile valley. Its principal village, Lorton, comprises two adjacent parts, Low Lorton and High Lorton. As a whole it is becoming a very popular place for week-end cottages, but it is still very much a village. Lorton Hall, in Low Lorton, has a pele-tower, said to be haunted by a woman who walks with a lighted candle, and two priest holes. King Malcolm III (1057–93) stayed at the Hall with his queen while touring his kingdom of Strathclyde. Nearby is 'The Wheatsheaf Inn'. The church, dedicated to St. Cuthbert, is between Low and High Lorton, but nearer the former. It was built

The village of Leece which occurs in Domesday as 'Lies'

Swarthmoor Hall became closely connected with the Quaker movement when George Fox married Margaret Fell, whose home it was, in 1669

Beetham, a quiet and attractive village. Effigies in the church were defaced by Cromwellian soldiers

Grayrigg, the home of one of the earliest Quakers, Francis Howgill

The footbridge at Stainton, near Crooklands, which had a working corn mill until 1951

The post office at Beetham, dated 1881

in 1887 on the site of an older church. It has a pinnacled tower and some interesting tombstones. One stone, just inside the churchyard gate, in memory of Daniel Fisher, expresses the admirable sentiment:

On Tombstones Praise is vainly spent,
Good works are Man's best monument.

Inside the church, the most prominent feature is the richly coloured window showing a group around the empty tomb of Christ. Pevsner calls it 'indefensible' and I am inclined to agree with him. There is also a long-handled collecting-shovel dated 1851. The tiny school next to the church was enlarged in 1887. The school in High Lorton bears the dates 1809, 1859 and 1895. The house next door (presumably the master's house) was built to commemorate the Diamond Jubilee of Queen Victoria. The post office-store is in High Lorton, as is 'The Horseshoe Inn', the Wesleyan chapel (1840), now the Methodist chapel, and the village hall, the Yew Tree Hall. At the back of the Hall is the famous yew tree beside which George Fox stood and preached Quakerism. It was immortalized by Wordsworth:

There is a yew-tree, pride of Lorton Vale,
Which to this day stands single in the midst
Of its own darkness, as it stood of yore.

Near it is a house dated 1733.

Loweswater is a scattered village, with the famous 'Kirkstile Inn' as its focal point. Beside the inn is the church of St. Bartholomew, built by the inhabitants in 1827 and restored in 1884. It is not particularly attractive either inside or out. The east end forms quite a pleasant apse. It has no stained glass. The first chapel was probably as early as the twelfth century. Not far away is the 1839 school with bell-cote and bell, with the village hall attached. There is a wonderful panorama of hills all around. Loweswater means 'leafy lake', and woods do come down to the edge of the lake.

From Loweswater, Buttermere is reached along the side of Crummock Water with all the splendour of mountain scenery around. The village is little more than a church, two inns, a store and a few farms. Right opposite the village are the waterfalls of Sourmilk Gill, tumbling down from Bleaberry Tarn. The tiny church perches picturesquely at the side of the road. It is dedicated to St. James, and was built in 1840 near the site of the old chapel. It was re-furnished in 1929–30 and the sanctuary paved with Honister slate. The porch was added in 1933. The font-cover was given by the village school-children in 1930. Sixteen carved wooden angels look down from the ceiling. The east window, showing Martha, is by Henry Holiday (1839–1927) and was installed in 1893. The porch gate is an interesting example of wrought-iron work, depicting a hill shepherd with sheep. The bell-turret has twin bells. 'The Bridge Hotel' is beside the road, and set back a little is 'The Fish Hotel', once the home of Mary Robinson, the Beauty of Buttermere. She achieved national fame when, after being deceived into marriage by the forger James Hatfield in 1802, she became his widow when he was hanged in Carlisle the following year. She married Richard Harrison, a farmer, in 1808, had quite a large family, and died in 1834. She is buried in Caldbeck churchyard.

Mockerkin is a small, grey, rather neglected village, built round a triangle. One lintel is dated 1660. Mockerkin Tarn, nearby, carried the legend common to so many of these village tarns—that it covers the site of an earlier village and castle.

The very scattered village of Lamplugh spreads from the A5086 road to the lanes around the church. It contains 'The Lamplugh Arms', the Women's Institute, 'The Pack of Hounds Inn', the very isolated post office (which is the former Lamplugh Mill on the Workington Road), and Lamplugh Hall, now a farm but still with its (renewed) 1595 stone above the entrance arch. The village is known for its 'sweet meat pie', and for 'Lamplugh pudding', which is not a dessert but is eaten hot by the hill farmers after long spells out in the cold weather. At one time the whole of this countryside was covered with trees, giving rise to the couplet:

> A squirrel could hop from tree to tree
> From Lamplugh Fells to Moresby.

A lych-gate green with lichen leads into the churchyard. The church walls are also lichen-covered. Perhaps Lamplugh gets more than its share of wet weather, an assumption reinforced by an umbrella-stand at the end of every pew. The memorial to the fallen of both World Wars stands in the churchyard at the west end of the church. At the east end is a group of three demon gargoyles. There is a double bell-cote with two bells. The church is dedicated to St. Michael and was restored and enlarged in 1870. The old font is beside the new one. The panelling around the nave is a memorial to two men killed during the 1914–18 war, and a third who died later as a result of the war. Down a lane not far from the church are a pair of semi-detached cottages bearing a plaque: 'In memory of two gallant English gentlemen'. They are also in memory of the two men killed at Hooge and Le Plantin (the names given to the cottages).

Winding roads, through lovely scenery, lead to the small, quiet village of Ennerdale Bridge on the river Ehen, meaning 'water'. There is a post office-store, the village school, 'The Fox and Hounds' inn, a few houses and farms and some new bungalows. St. Mary's church stands quietly off the road, rather hidden in a clump of trees. A medieval chapel stood on the spot until 1857, when it was demolished and the present church built. Wordsworth's poem 'The Brothers' was written after a visit to the old chapel in 1799. The bell in the little round bell-tower on the south-east corner is from the old chapel, and bears the inscription '*Sancta Bega ora pro nobis*'—St. Bega pray for us. A relative of Wordsworth's, John Wordsworth, was the incumbent from 1874–6.

Ponsonby village is on the east side of the A595 and comprises a very few houses, one dated 1774, in a cul-de-sac. Ponsonby church is west of the road on a hill top, looking over miles of fields and surrounded by a shallow, dry moat. The only defensive purpose of this moat is to keep animals out of the churchyard. The church, of unknown dedication, is ancient but was in so bad a state in 1874 that it had to be completely restored. The east window by Morris & Co. was put in at this time. It represents the Crucifixion and Nativity, with Saints Peter, John, Paul and Barnabas at the sides. Most intriguing, however, is the monument to Thomas Curwen who died in 1653. It is in the sanctuary beside the altar, and shows two men with beards, shorts, buttoned coats, and bowler hats. One is digging; the other is leaning on a skull—

presumably representing labour and rest! The west window is by Henry Holiday (1839–1927), depicting Faith and Charity. There are many memorial tablets to the Stanleys, who have lived at the Manor for many centuries.

One of the best-known villages in this area is Gosforth, 'goose ford'. It is now almost a small town, with a number of small shops and a fair amount of new housing development. It has amongst its older houses one dated 1628—only twenty-nine years after 115 of the 600 people living in the parish died of the plague. It can boast three inns—'The Horse and Groom', 'Ye Olde Lion and Lamb', and 'The Wheatsheaf Inn'. There is a Wesleyan chapel dated 1874, a school (1886), and a village hall (1930). The church, of St. Mary, retains some of its Norman work, but was restored in 1789 and substantially again in 1896–9. During its history it has belonged to the Dioceses of York, of Chester, and, since 1854, of Carlisle. It is a pleasant, airy church with a bell-tower with three bells. There are interesting carved faces supporting the chancel arch. The Chinese bell on the west windowsill was captured at Anunkry, a fort on the river Canton, in 1841. The church is famous for the large number of Anglo-Saxon and Danish remains it possesses, the most important being the fourteen-foot-high tenth-century cross in the churchyard. Also in the churchyard is a cork tree planted in 1833 and probably the most northerly specimen in England.

On the road from Gosforth to Wastwater is the village of Strands, set in a wooded hollow with mountain views. The maypole on the village green was erected in 1897 to commemorate the sixty years' reign of Queen Victoria. It took the place of an old oak tree. There is a drinking-fountain dated 1880, and two inns—'The Screes Hotel' and 'Strands Hotel'. The village hall is next door to the low, dales-type church, the parish church of Nether Wasdale. Its nave and chancel are one. The slightly ornate ceiling has texts on it, and fourteen little cherubs' heads look down from above. The panelling by the altar, and the carvings of the pulpit and lectern, are from York Minster. The alms-box stands on a cherub's head. The Royal Arms of George III are in relief, the only ones I can remember seeing in quite that form. The east window is a memorial to the four men of the parish who were killed in the

1914–18 war. The remains of painted lettering can be seen on the south wall.

Wasdale Head, the climbers' village, is reached by a road that runs along the lake-side, with some of the most spectacular scenery anywhere in England. It is hardly a village as such, but it has a church and 'The Wasdale Hotel'. The tiny church is one of the smallest in England, although not *the* smallest; I believe that distinction belongs to Culbone Church in Somerset. Wasdale church has an east window 'in memory of the happy and prosperous reign of Her Majesty Queen Victoria', and possesses Victorian iron brackets for oil lamps. There was no right of burial in the churchyard before 1889. It now contains the graves of many climbers, some of whom met their deaths in the neighbourhood. The old pack-horse bridge, widened slightly to take one car at a time, is known as 'Down-in-the-Dale Bridge'.

North-west of Kendal is the sizeable village of Burneside. It consists mainly of fairly recent houses, and it doubtless serves as a dormitory suburb for Kendal (only two miles away), although quite a number of people will be employed at Croppers Paper Mills. This mill has been making paper since about 1833, and was bought as a going concern by James Cropper in 1845. Opposite the mill is a private house which at one time was part of the old school. The 1885 school still stands in the street leading to the mill, but has been replaced by a new school. The post office is tucked away rather oddly behind the Bryce Institute, opened in 1898. There is an 1872 drinking-fountain, no longer in use, and in front of sixteen houses built in memory of Charles and Edith Cropper, is an armillary sundial. The pub is 'The Jolly Anglers'. St. Oswald's church tells the story of the village's increasing population. It was originally a tiny chapel, founded some centuries ago, but was superseded by a small Gothic building in 1826. In 1861 a south aisle was added, to cater for the growing village, and in 1869 a wing was added on the north by James Cropper in memory of his wife. In 1880 further extensive alterations took place and the nave and south aisle were entirely rebuilt to produce the present large church. This is built, like many of the houses, of Westmorland slates. The 1936 east window is interesting. It shows St. Oswald planting the cross before the fight on 'Heavenfield'

Hexham; and at the other side is St. Kentigern in Cumbria, with below him the saint as a boy with the robin he is said to have brought back to life after boys had killed it. Also worthy of inspection are the locally-made carved reredos, the unusual paintings in the Bateman Memorial window in the south aisle, and the carving of the Virgin and Child in the nave.

More or less at the end of a long cul-de-sac, in the lonely depths of the wild and lovely country of the Kentmere valley, is the small village of Kentmere—more a scattering of houses and farms than a community. It possesses a village hall dated 1925, and nearby is a base of the Mountain Rescue Team. The plain, cement-surfaced church of St. Cuthbert has sixteenth-century roof-beams, but was restored in 1866 and again renovated in 1950. It is in a way reminiscent of Bewcastle church. The original oil lamps hang from the wooden ceiling, but have electric bulbs inside them. There is no stained glass. The long altar, with its rather crudely painted front, has two almost 'fairground' kneeling angels guarding it—one on each side. The bronze memorial tablet to Bernard Gilpin (1517–83), 'the Apostle of the North', was made by the Keswick School of Industrial Arts in 1901.[1] He was born at Kentmere Hall, now a farm. The lake, or 'mere', was drained during the second half of last century and diatomite is dug there and used industrially by the Cape Asbestos Company. It is the only workable diatomaceous deposit in England. In 1955 a wooden boat was discovered, probably 1,000 years old. It is now in the National Maritime Museum.

Troutbeck church is on the main Windermere to Penrith road. It is The Jesus Chapel, and is simple and rather lonely-looking. The entry is through the 1736 tower and under the balcony at the west end. The clock in the tower was inserted in 1897. A chapel was first built at the end of the fifteenth century, and was consecrated in 1562 by the then Archbishop of Canterbury. It was re-built in 1736 and re-furnished in 1861. The Royal Arms above the door are of George II, 1737. The sixteenth- and seventeenth-century carved woodwork in the chancel is from Calgarth Hall near Lake Windermere. The dominating feature, however, is the 1873

[1] Gilpin, made Archdeacon of Durham in 1556, spent much of his time on missionary journeys in the wilds of Cumberland and Northumberland.

east window, the joint work of Edward Burne-Jones, William Morris and Ford Madox Brown. Burne-Jones is said to have been working on the window when his two friends, by chance on a fishing holiday, decided to help him. The five main figures, including the young, clean-shaven Christ, are by Burne-Jones. The foliage which gives an unusual amount of green in the window is by Morris. Opposite the church is a small school, and nearby is the Queen Victoria Jubilee drinking fountain. A caravan-site is by the Trout beck. The picturesque village is spread along about a mile of narrow hilly road, running almost parallel with the main road and looking down on it. There are several old houses—one of them, Townend, has belonged to the National Trust since 1947 and houses a sort of village museum—and a post office. The 1689 inn is oddly named 'The Mortal Man', but was originally 'The White House'. It had formerly an inn-sign painted by the artist Julius Caesar Ibbotson (1759–1817) who lived in Troutbeck for a short period at the beginning of the last century. The sign showed on one side fat, jolly Nat Fleming, and on the other side pale, thin Ned Partridge, with the words:

O mortal man, that lives by bread,
What is it makes thy nose so red?
Thou silly fool, that looks't so pale,
'Tis drinking Sally Birkett's ale.

Unfortunately the sign disappeared many years ago and has never been recovered. Its modern replacement is a poor imitation.

Nestling in the rugged Langdale Valley and with mountains all around is Elterwater, taking its name 'swan lake' from its small lake. Its pub is 'The Britannia', and it has one or two shops. Green slate is abundant in the area and most of the buildings are made from it. The Langdale Bowling Club has a green in the village. On the village green is a six-sided seat.

The village of Langdale is Chapel Stile. Its older houses are of slate, and it has a good number of recent houses. There is 'The Langdales Hotel', the Church of England school, a post office-store, and a showroom of Langdale Woodcraft. A public shelter is in memory of King George V. The surprisingly large church, dedicated to the Holy Trinity, was built in 1857 to replace the old chapel of 1750. It stands at the foot of Silverhow (1,292 ft.) and has no windows on the north side, probably because the dark hillside comes down steeply quite close to it. The east window is a poor imitation of the Troutbeck window by Burne-Jones. There is, however, an interesting modern window of St. Francis on the south side. The rolls of honour for the Boer War and both World Wars are in the church. At the side of the street outside the church is an 1887 drinking fountain to commemorate the 50th year of Victoria's reign. Langdale means, simply, 'long valley'.

This chapter ends with short notes about two of the best-known villages in the county. Rydal has been somewhat overshadowed by its near neighbour Grasmere, but it is still much visited by the thousands of Wordsworth fans. Everywhere in this district is reminiscent of the Wordsworths, de Quincey, and Hartley Coleridge. The latter, much loved by Wordsworth, spent the last eleven years of his life in Nab Cottage. Before that it had been the home of the girl with whom de Quincey fell in love. It still stands, with the date 1702 above its door, beside the high road half way along Rydal Water. Wordsworth lived for almost half his lifetime at Rydal Mount not far from the church. The field Wordsworth gave to his daughter, now known as Dora's Field, is behind the church and can be reached through the churchyard. It was given to the National Trust some forty years ago. The not particularly attractive church of St. Mary was built in 1824. It has three windows of interest, all in the south wall. One is the 1891 Quillinan Memorial window of child angels, the work of Henry Holiday (1839–1927). Another is a window to Wilson Fox (d. 1887), who was Physician-in-Ordinary to Queen Victoria. The third is to the memory of Dr. Thomas Arnold (1795–1842), Headmaster of Rugby School, and a friend of the Wordsworths. The Arnold family pew was the one in front of the lectern; that of the Wordsworths the one in front of the pulpit. The name Rydal means 'the valley where rye was grown'.

Grasmere, 'the grassy shore of the lake', must be one of the best-known villages in the English-speaking world. If there is any-one who does not know of it from its Wordsworthian connection, or as the centre for the Lake Poets, he will probably have heard of its rush-bearing ceremony, or its sports, or just of its own natural beauty. Its sports include fell-running, hound-trails, Cumberland and Westmorland-style wrestling, and athletics. In the Guides Race the runners reach a height of 966 feet. The rush-bearing takes place on the nearest Saturday to St. Oswald's Day, 5th August. After the service the children receive the traditional reward of a piece of Grasmere gingerbread. The village is geared to accommodate and cater for visitors, with its gift shops, artists' studios, etc. Dove Cottage, with its Wordsworth museum, is at one end of the village, 'The Swan Inn' at the other. It was to this inn that Sir Walter Scott went for his morning dram when staying with the abstemious Wordsworth. The church is dedicated to St. Oswald. It has a wooden alms-box carved with the date 1648 and the words 'S. Oswaldus Poor Box'. In the north wall is stained glass showing the raising of Lazarus, done in 1893 by Henry Holiday (1839–1927). In addition to the graves of William and Mary Wordsworth and other members of the Wordsworth family, the churchyard contains the grave of Hartley Coleridge (whom Wordsworth wished to have buried near him). Also a memorial to the poet Arthur Hugh Clough (1819–61), who is actually buried in Florence, and the grave of Sir John Richardson (1787–1865), the distinguished Arctic explorer. It also has several yew trees planted by Wordsworth in 1819. Beside the northern or lych-gate is the gingerbread shop which was, until 1854, the village school.

10

The Southern Lake District

THIS chapter moves south to softer, more wooded country, to Windermere and Coniston Water. Most of the villages lie either between these two lakes, or to the east of Windermere.

Crook, on the B5284, is a village with no real centre. The church and the pub are about one mile apart. The pub is 'The Sun Inn', and along a side road not far away the former Independent chapel, 1866, is now a private house. The school, built in 1873, and the 1914–18 War Memorial Hall are to the west. A little farther westwards is the church of St. Catherine, built in 1887. The tower of the older church is still standing, and can be seen on a hill to the south-west; it can be reached by a short walk across the fields. The present church seems too large for the scattered community it serves. It is rather bleak and barn-like, with no stained glass. There is a memorial tablet in the church to the five men who died in both World Wars.

Another spread-out village is Underbarrow, so named from being at the foot of Helsington Barrow. The pub is 'The Punch Bowl'. A house dated 1854 has in its garden a model of itself, made of Westmorland slate and complete with television aerial. The village is famous for the tastiness of its pheasants. The church, of All Saints, is at the northern end of the village. It is cruciform, built in 1869 on the site of earlier churches, and has little of particular interest. The old oil lamps which once lit it during services are still hanging from the roof, but electric lighting is now used. The war memorial is on a mound outside the church. The school is nearby. The Quaker, Edward Burrough, was born at Underbarrow; he met George Fox when he was nineteen, and became a member of the

Society of Friends. His parents turned him out of their home and he travelled about preaching. He died in Newgate Prison at the age of twenty-eight. According to local belief, one of the survivors of the famous Charge of the Light Brigade lived in the village. Brigster Woods, on the Levens road, are now National Trust property.

The very hilly, windy village shown on the map as Church Town is more generally known as Crosthwaite, and includes Crosthwaite Green. Its pub is another 'Punch Bowl'. The church hall and church are behind it. The church, dedicated to St. Mary, was rebuilt in 1878–9. It is very long, and without side aisles. The stained glass in the apse at the east end was put in at the same time as the rebuilding was done, and the font was given by the builders and workmen. The painted reredos above and around the altar was added in 1885, and is interesting. A bust of William Pearson (1780–1856), in the church, gives no clue that he was a close friend of the Wordsworths nor that he was the author of a work on the *Natural history of Crosthwaite and Lythe, and the valley of the Winster*. He was born at Crosthwaite. There is a post office-store, a large memorial hall, and a school. The earliest school was founded by George Cocke in 1665.

Not far from the shore of Lake Windermere is a group of quiet grey-and-white houses making up the village of Winster, 'the left one', almost on the old North Lancashire border. Many of the houses are old. The post office-store is dated 1600. There is a small school. The pub is 'The Brown Horse Inn', and down a lane opposite to it is the grey church of Westmorland slate; a small church set away from the village amongst trees. The war memorial in the churchyard is under a chestnut tree. The church is dedicated to the Holy Trinity and was rebuilt in 1875. Its windows are very attractive inside. The east window contains stained glass, and so does one in the south wall. This is a modern (1941) depiction of St. Kentigern with a robin perched on his forefinger. A pitch-pipe, exhibited in a glass case, was last used about 1860 by the village blacksmith, who was also the Clerk.

Levens Bridge is the well-known junction where the A590 to Barrow meets the A6. Levens village, 'leafy ridge', lies north-west of the junction, off both the main roads. It is a large village with several shops in addition to the post office-general store. Much of it is new, or fairly new. It has an 1892 Wesleyan chapel, now the Methodist church; 'The Hare and Hounds' inn; and the Levens Institute, opened in 1903 to commemorate the coronation of Edward VII. A lych-gate leads to the grey stone church with its sharp-pointed spire. The war memorial stands at the south-east corner. The churchyard was not consecrated until 1913, but the church, dedicated to St. John the Evangelist, was built in 1828. Better known than the village is Levens Hall, south of Levens Bridge. It is one of the largest Elizabethan houses in the north, and possesses the finest topiary work in the country. The garden was laid out by the French gardener to King James II, Monsieur Beaumont, who also laid out the gardens at Hampton Court. He planted the famous oak avenue at Levens Hall; one and a half miles long, and the subject of a hotly contested inquiry when the motorway link was being planned.

Witherslack means 'wooded valley', and it is today a group of grey houses huddled together in lovely wooded scenery. It is famous for its Witherslack damsons. There is a post office, store and village hall. The church and school are quite a way out of the village on the Newton road. The church of St. Paul was built under the terms of the will of John Barwick (1612–64) and consecrated in 1671. It was extensively restored in 1861. It is a very pleasant, nicely proportioned church. The very little stained glass is in part of the 1671 east window. In the north-east corner is the carving of a baby who died aged one-and-a-half. The baptistry was added in 1960. The Royal Arms are of Queen Anne, 1710. The fine canopied pulpit was once a three-decker, and is beautifully carved. The church tower has a one-handed clock, 1768, on its south face. The 1757 sundial in the churchyard has a hardly-legible dial with the initials J.B. (John Barwick) and the date 1671. John Barwick was a very loyal and active Royalist, and was at one time committed to the Tower. After the Restoration he was offered the Bishopric of Carlisle, but declined. He became Dean of St. Paul's, and was buried there. His younger brother, Peter (1619–1705), was physician to Charles II. He refused to leave London during the plague, preferring to stay and help the sick. His home was destroyed during the Great Fire. All his life he worked unremittingly for the poor, without fee. His sight failed in 1694. Both John and Peter were born in Witherslack, and there are panels bearing both their arms in the church. Dean Barwick's School, founded 1678, and the Master's House, are outside the church gate. The school was re-built in 1874.

Winding, undulating roads lead to Cartmell Fell through deserted, wooded scrubland. The name means 'sandbank by rocky ground' and the few scattered farms and houses appear to have been thrown down at random amongst the out-croppings of rock. 'Hodge Hill' would seem to be the village's licensed house. The delightful little church was built about 1504, and claims to be the only one in the north-west of England dedicated to St. Anthony. The floor of the church slopes downward towards the altar. The fifteenth-century stained glass in the east window is fascinating. A tombstone not far away tells that:

> Underneath this stone A mould'ring Virgin lies
> Who was the Pleasure once of Human Eyes. . .

She was little Betty Poole, aged three. There is a 1698 three-decker pulpit, and sixteenth- and seventeenth-century pews. On the south wall is a picture, in tiles, of St. Anthony. In the vestry is one of only two pre-Reformation crucifix figures in England. It is a wooden sculpture of the crucified Christ from the large crucifix which would have surmounted the old chancel screen, probably thirteenth-century, and about two feet six inches high. Princess Margaret visited this lonely church in 1958, and her aunt, the Princess Royal, in 1963. It appears in Mrs Humphry Ward's novel *Helbeck of Bannisdale* as 'Browhead chapel'.

Almost at the southernmost tip of Windermere is Staveley, 'the wood where staves were obtained'. It is a small cluster of houses huddled together inside a triangle of roads. The 1875 school has separate entrances for boys and girls. Next to it is the church, dating from the seventeenth century. Inscriptions above the east window, and one in the north wall, show that it was restored in 1678. The south aisle was added and the tower built in 1793. Major restorations took place in 1896–7, when the church was dedicated to St. Mary—it is not known to whom it was dedicated earlier. The lych-gate was erected in 1927 in memory of those who fell in the 1914–18 war, but now includes also the fallen in the 1939–45 war. Mrs Mary Dixon was a great benefactress of both church and village. She was the daughter of John Smeaton, of Eddystone lighthouse fame. Edmund Law (1703–87), Bishop of Carlisle, was born in Staveley.

Nearby Newby Bridge consists of very little more than the fine seventeenth-century bridge, and the eighteenth-century 'Swan Hotel'. The village caters mainly for the passing tourist trade.

Another village of scattered houses and farms, with a small nucleus clustered near the surprisingly large church, is Finsthwaite. The church is dedicated to St. Peter, and its spire is surmounted by a fish. It was built in 1873 on the site of an earlier, 1724, one. It contains some rather nice stained glass and a mosaic reredos. The ceiling is partly painted. In a case near the communion rail are a cross, a cup, and two patens. All were made by soldiers in northern Italy during the 1914–18 war so that the padre could celebrate communion on Christmas Day. He later became vicar at this church. Above them is a bronze tablet in memory of the fallen of the 1939–45 war. Beside the church is the school, 1874. In the churchyard, its inscription not easily read, is a plain cross to 'Clementina Johannes Sobiesky Douglass, of Waterside', who died in May 1771. She was most probably Prince Charles Edward Stuart's natural daughter by his mistress Clementina Walkenshaw. When I saw the cross, a few small sprigs of white heather wilted at its base.

Bouth is a fairly large residential village, with a post office-store, and the 'White Hart' inn. The old schoolhouse is now a private house. The steep hill of Ridding Side separates the village from Spark Bridge, where they still carry on the old trade of bobbin-making, combined at Spark Bridge Mill with the making of reels, and with wrought-iron work. The pub is 'The Royal Oak'. There is a Wesleyan chapel dated 1863; and, beside the Broughton-in-Furness road, the fourteenth-century 'Farmers Arms' (originally a farmhouse) with its spinning gallery, which identifies itself with Lowick although it appears to be a part of Spark Bridge.

'Lowick, 'leafy bay', is a scattered community, some of it near the road leading northwards to Coniston Water, some of it clustered round the church. Oak baskets, or swills, used to be made by the local people. The pub is 'The Red Lion Inn', and if the signboard is to be accepted, 'The Farmers Arms' (mentioned above at Spark Bridge) is also in Lowick. The Sunday school and reading room, next to the church, is used as a village hall. The church, dedicated to St. Luke, was re-built in 1884–5 on the site where a chapel had stood from before 1577. On its south wall is an 1828 sundial. The glass in the east window is colourful, although not particularly attractive. Below it is a carved-oak reredos. A sacrament-type lamp is kept burning in the sanctuary, from whence it can be seen for miles over the common, and acts as a guiding light.

There is little to see in the small village of large houses that is Colton except its church, and that is worth seeing. It is set away (almost hidden) from the village, eastwards up a steep hill. Beside the footpath approaching the church is a well traditionally known as St. Cuthbert's well, and used for baptisms. Farther up the hill past the church is the village hall and almost opposite a 1767 mounting-block, or horsing stone. The church, dedicated to the Holy Trinity, is in a wonderful setting. It is itself a delightful church, surprisingly large inside. A chapel, connected with Furness Abbey and served by its monks, existed in the fifteenth century, probably about 1485. After the Dissolution it was enlarged, and it was consecrated in 1578 by Archbishop Sandys, who was born at Satterthwaite in the heart of the Grizedale Forest to the north. The church was re-built about 1600, the north transept was added in 1721, and the vestry in 1762. Further restorations took place in 1840, 1890 and, recently, in 1952–3. The Royal Arms are of George III. There is a wall-clock made in Ulverston in 1829, and in a case a copy of the Bishop's Bible of 1577, sometimes referred to as the 'treacle Bible' because it reads, in Jeremiah 8. 22. —'Is there no tryacle at Gilead?' The north wall has some interesting modern stained glass, but most of the other stained glass is in very poor condition. From outside the church, the varying level of the windows is very noticeable. In the churchyard is a sundial dated 1764, on an 1886 base.

The concentrated little village of Oxen Park has a post office, a licensed house, the 'Manor House', a telephone kiosk, and virtually nothing else. From there the road winds through beautiful wooded country into Grizedale Forest, and to a clearing where is Satterthwaite—'the clearing by a shieling'. The post office is the village store, the inn is 'The Eagles Head'. The village hall is opposite the church—one of the warmest in winter that I know. It is a pleasant, unremarkable church built in 1835 and restored in 1888. A church existed in 1577 and was re-built in 1675 to give way to the present one. In the porch is an old, iron-bound chest. The 1910 east window looks mid-Victorian. Edwin Sandys (1519–88) was born at Satterthwaite. He strongly supported the principles of the Reformation and was imprisoned in the Tower by Queen Mary. He was later one of the bishops appointed to produce a new translation of the Bible. He became Bishop of London and, in 1576, Archbishop of York.

At the northern end of the clearing in Grizedale Forest is Grizedale itself; meaning 'pigs' valley'. It contains the Wild Life Centre and 'The Theatre in the Forest', opened in 1970. The Theatre was presenting 'The Barber of Seville' when I visited the village. Grizedale Forest Handicrafts is a cottage industry for which articles are made in the homes, and beside the firesides, of local people. Such items as deer skin handbags and moccasins are very popular; they are made from skins obtained from the Forestry Commission's annual deer cull. A special dish of these parts is said to be 'Grey Squirrel stew'. Grizedale Hall was a prisoner-of-war camp in the 1939–45 war. Franz von Werra, the only German prisoner-of-war to get back to his own country, was held there for a time and made an unsuccessful attempt at escape from there.

The village of Sawrey, 'a muddy place', comprises Near and Far Sawrey, made up for the most part of large houses well spread out. Near Sawrey is best known for Beatrix Potter's house at Hill Top, near the shore of Esthwaite Water. The house is open to the public from Easter to the end of October. Nearby is 'The Tower Bank Arms'. At Far Sawrey is 'The Sawrey Hotel'; the post office; a store selling Beatrix Potter china; and Braithwaite Hall school. It also has the church of St. Peter (nothing to do, of course, with Peter Rabbit!). It is a large, cruciform church built in 1867–9, and possesses some fairly interesting stained glass, including a rather unusual window of the Good Samaritan.

The tiny village of Colthouse, within sight of Hawkshead, is where Wordsworth lodged for a time while attending Hawkshead Grammar School, after Ann Tyson and her husband moved from Hawkshead to Colthouse in 1783. In the village, in excellent condition, is the 1688 Friends' Meeting House, with the date above its door.

High and Low Wray are on the western shore of Lake Windermere. The village hall and club is at High Wray; the church and castle at Low Wray. Each place has a few houses. The church, dedicated to St. Margaret, appears to be kept locked. It has an 1856 sundial over its porch. The massive tower gives the appearance of having been added later. It was built entirely at the expense of Dr. James Dawson, a Liverpool surgeon, who also built the neighbouring Wray castle between 1840 and 1847. It is said that during its building the frost was so severe that building materials for it were carted across the frozen surface of the lake. The castle is now National Trust property, and used as a Training College for merchant navy radio/electronics officers. The public have access to the grounds and lake shore.

Coniston, at the western head of Coniston Water, means 'the king's manor'. It has quite a number of shops, hotels, etc. (including the former coaching inn 'The Black Bull' where Turner stayed in 1797), and could be considered almost a small town. The Old Man of Coniston (2,635 ft.) towers above it to the west. The Roman Catholic church, dedicated to the Sacred Heart of Jesus, was built in 1872 beside the road to the south. The Methodist church was originally the 1875 Wesleyan chapel. The Anglican church of St. Andrew is built on the site of a chapel built by William Fleming in 1586, and pulled down in 1818. The present church was built in 1819, but thoroughly restored, and the chancel and vestry added, in 1891. It has an unusual version of the Royal Arms on the balcony front. Of special interest is the Fleming brass of 1680, and a baptistry window by C. E. Kempe. Outside the church is the war memorial to the fallen in both World Wars, with a special stone in memory of a man who won the V.C., and died in 1963. What brings many visitors to the churchyard, however, is the grave of John Ruskin (1819–1900), buried there in preference to a national grave in Westminster Abbey. The Anglo-Saxon type cross made of local Tilberthwaite stone is in the north-east corner of the churchyard. There is a Ruskin Museum not far away, and Brantwood, where he lived from 1871, is about one-and-a-half miles south-east, on the other side of the lake. Two men have made Coniston Water famous, in very different ways. It was, of course, the stretch of water where Donald Campbell met his death in January 1967 while attempting to break the world water-speed record. It is also the principal setting for Arthur Ransome's classic children's adventure stories, including *Swallows and Amazons*.

Similarly overlooked by the Old Man of Coniston is Torver, 'peat shieling'. It possesses a post office and a store. On one side of the church is 'The Church House Inn', and on the other side the 1872 school, with a large bell behind wire mesh. The 1920 lych-gate opposite the church is a memorial to those who fell in both World Wars. A twelfth-century chapel originally stood on the site of the present church. Until 1538 the dead had to be carried through all types of weather to Ulverston, sixteen miles away. In that year Archbishop Cranmer granted a deed of consecration permitting burials at the chapel burial ground. A new church was built in 1849, to be replaced by the present church of St. Luke in 1883–4. The strong central tower has a windvane in the shape of a large green fish. The font is ancient. In the sanctuary is a 1707 collecting scoop. Above a plaque to the war dead is another, dated 1727, telling of the gift of £15 'for the use of the Poor of Torver as to paying for Learning and Books'.

Southwards from Torver the winding road leads through lovely wooded country, at times alongside Coniston Water, to Blawith, 'black forest'. Despite its two churches it is not much of a village today. There is a post office; but the school, re-built in 1859, is no longer in use. On the west side of the road are the pathetic ruins of the old chapel, built about 1560 and now hidden behind a few trees with its tombstones overgrown with brambles. Not quite opposite, on the other side of the road, is the 1863 church of St John the Baptist. The churchyard is entered under a 1922 lych-gate. Inside the church is a chest hollowed out of a log. The chancel was built by public subscription. The war memorial plaque, and a shelf with flowers, are underneath a window depicting St. George and St. Michael. It is said that in 1781 it was agreed to build a steeple thirty feet high and that the bell to go in it should be paid for by the sale of Blea Brow. This would be for the old church of course, and it gave rise to some contemporary verse:

Blawith poor people,
An old church and new steeple,
As poor as hell,
They had to sell
A bit of fell
To buy a bell,
Blawith poor people.

Grizebeck, 'pigs' brook', is a small community with a rather run-down air. It has 'The Greyhound Inn', and a school, and the 1899 Mission church of Kirkby-in-Furness, but is of small interest.

A winding, hilly road runs above the lovely tree-lined valley of the Duddon, and leads into some of the most uninhabited parts of the whole of Cumbria. One of its two villages is Ulpha, or 'wolf hill'. There is not much of a village, and its farms are scattered on the fell-sides. It has a post office-store, a row of Gunson Almshouses dated 1914, a village hall, and 'The Travellers Rest Hotel'. The small, whitewashed church is dedicated to St. John the Baptist. It is a delightful, barn-shaped church dating originally from about 1415 but restored and re-seated in 1882. Wall paintings with the date 1793 were discovered in 1934. One shows the Royal Arms of Queen Anne. There is no stained glass. The east window is probably seventeenth century. The polished brass reredos was the work of a former incumbent. Electric lighting has been fitted into the old oil lamps.

Seathwaite is surrounded on all sides by mountains—Harter Fell (2,140 ft.) and Grey Friar (2,536 ft.) to the north; Caw (1,735 ft.) to the south; eastwards are the Old Man of Coniston (2,635 ft.) and Brown Pike (2,237 ft.); while to the west are Worm Crag (1,400 ft.) and Hesk Fell (1,566 ft.). There is a village hall, and 'The Newfield Hotel', but no longer a post office. The Church of the Holy Trinity replaced an earlier one, in 1874. Ruskin tried to save the old chapel from being pulled down, but failed. Wordsworth wrote a sonnet about it. The present church is small, but obviously loved. Its Royal Arms are of George I. There is a brass tablet to Robert Walker and his wife, both of whom lived to be almost ninety-three years old. Walker (1709–1802), was parson of the old church for sixty-seven years. His name has become something of a legend, and he is referred to as 'Wonderful Walker'. He was priest, teacher, doctor, scholar and helper to all his parishioners; he worked hard to bring up a family of twelve children, turning his hand to almost everything; and at his death he left a small fortune. Just outside the church porch is a stone used by him as a stool when clipping sheep. Nearby is his tombstone.

11

Furness and Cartmel

THE villages in this chapter lie between the Kent Estuary and the Duddon Estuary, and south of the busy road which joins Levens Bridge and Broughton-in-Furness. Most of them were formerly in North Lancashire, but now come into the county of Cumbria.

The only Westmorland village covered by this chapter is Meathop —'the piece of firm land in the fens'. It is but a cluster of lovely old grey stone farms, with a few more modern houses and a little building still going on, near the hospital which was originally built as a convalescent home in 1891. The church which serves the village is at Witherslack, north of the main road.

Lindale, 'lime tree valley', is a large village lying along, and to the south of, the main Barrow road, the A590. It has steep hills in almost every direction with grey houses perched at all conceivable angles. There are two pubs, 'The Lindale Inn' and 'The Royal Oak', with a post office between them. Apart from the church, its most interesting feature is the ugly iron obelisk which stands on a mound close beside the B5277 where it turns off to Grange-over-Sands. It is in memory of John Wilkinson (1728–1808), the great iron-master, and bears a relief portrait of him. He lived at Castle Head to the south-east, and it was on the river Winster nearby that he launched the first iron ship ever to float, in 1786. It was only a model, but it was the forerunner of a new type of ship which was to break with the tradition of 'wooden walls'. Five years earlier Wilkinson had built our first iron bridge. He made a huge iron coffin for himself, and also the obelisk to serve as a tomb marker, and directed that he should be buried in his own garden. This was done, but later the family sold the house and the new owners had the remains removed to Lindale church. The obelisk was struck by lightning and lay neglected in the shrubbery for years until it was re-erected where it now stands. The church is up a steep hill past the large village hall with its big clock, and past the grey stone village school with its single bell-cote and bell. The school was first built in 1838 and enlarged in 1894. The church is dedicated to St. Paul. Its history is uncertain, but it is known to have been in existence in 1650, and George Fox, the Quaker, preached in it in 1652. The present church was built in 1828, and there is in the churchyard a massive monument to George Webster of Kendal who built it. The chancel was added in 1864, and the north aisle added in 1913. The Royal Arms above the door are of George III. There is an interesting carved and painted reredos of Christ flanked by two angels with St. Martin on one side of him and St. Elizabeth of Hungary on the other. A memorial tablet to John Wilkinson's wife, Mary, is on the south wall, probably above the spot where he was re-buried under the pews.

A couple of miles farther along the A590 is the village of High Newton, made up of little clumps of houses on either side of the road. The pub, 'The Crown Hotel', is on the north side. The private house opposite was formerly the Mission Hall, and the old school with its bell still hanging under a canopy became, in 1971, the new village hall. South of the main road a cluster of houses includes the post office-store; one house dated 1754 over its door; and another with a fall-pipe bearing the date 1765. The morning before George Fox preached at Lindale in 1652 he records that at Newton 'the multitude hauled me out, struck, and punched me, and threw me headlong over a stone wall'.

The tall spire of St. Peter's church, Field Broughton, crowned by its weathercock, is prominent for many miles around. It was consecrated in 1894, to replace an earlier one built nearby in 1745 and completely demolished in 1892. The churchyard is entered by a lych-gate. Above the church porch is a figure of St. Peter. The east window, by C. E. Kempe, depicts scenes from the saint's life, and gives a calm and pleasing effect to that end of the church. Under the 1921 war memorial windows is a plaque in honour of the six men who died during the 1939–45 war, with badges of their units. The pleasant, quiet village lies a short distance away, set back from the Cartmel road.

Allithwaite, 'the clearing of the Norseman Eilifr', is a large, mainly residential village, with much new and recent building. It has a post office-store and other shops; a village hall (1908); a Congregational church; and two inns, 'The Farmers Arms' and 'The Royal Oak'. The church of St. Mary was built in 1865 at the same time as the school and the vicarage. Its bell-turret supports a short spire. The stained glass in the church pays tribute to the men killed in the two World Wars. The east window, full of warriors in armour carrying swords, is to the dead of 1914–18; the window above the altar in the south chapel is to the fallen of the 1939–45 war. Beside this altar hang poppy wreaths from the preceding Armistice Day. From the church there is a fine view of Morecambe Bay, with Wraysholme Tower, now in ruins, keeping watch for marauders as it has done for five hundred years or more.

Also largely residential is Kents Bank, on the edge of the sands and geared to the holiday trade. It has a post office-store and a railway station, and commands a lovely view towards Silverdale. It was the north-western end of the over-sands route via Hest Bank to Lancaster—only one-third of the distance by road, and used daily by a coach until the building of the railway. Guides were available to conduct parties across but many perished, and in the churchyard at Cartmel are the graves of more than a hundred people who were drowned on the crossing. In 1857 a party of a dozen or so young men and women were overtaken by the tide on their way to the Lancaster hirings. The earliest guides were provided by the Priory at Cartmel. After the dissolution of the monasteries and until 1877 the guides were appointed and paid by the Duchy of Lancaster.

The old village of Flookburgh was once a market town. It was granted its first charter by Edward I in 1278. This was renewed by Henry IV in 1412, and again by Charles II in 1675. All these charters are referred to on the present market cross, which was erected in 1882 on the site of the original thirteenth-century one. A fire in 1686 destroyed much of the town, but houses still bearing the dates 1617, 1625, 1665 and 1686 must have escaped the blaze. There is a post office-store and several other shops. In the days of coach travel there were five inns, but now only 'The Hope and Anchor Inn' and 'The Crown Inn' are left. It was at 'The Crown Inn' that Charles II dined on a 'feast of cockles'. Cockle gathering and flat fishing (for flukes—hence the name?)[1] have been the major industries. The village is now spreading outwards, with recent housing development, and there is a new school. The church of St. John the Baptist was built in 1897–1900. Its unusual tower has a large fish (presumably a fluke) on its weathervane. It is a pleasant church with an apse at the east end. Its windows depict many saints, and its Royal Arms are of George III. In the church is preserved the charter of Charles II, together with the civic regalia of sword, staff and halberd. Also in the church is the Union Flag which was carried in front of Admiral Beatty at the Peace Parade in 1919. A hawthorn tree in the churchyard at the east end of the church was planted by Queen Mary in 1937.

Cark, 'rock or stone', is a compact little village overlooking Ulverston Sands. A few of its houses are down by the mill-stream. The Wesleyan chapel of 1904 is now the Methodist church. It has 'The Engine Inn' and 'The Rose and Crown Hotel', and several shops. George Fox was once held prisoner in Cark Hall, a late sixteenth-century house with mullioned windows. At Holker Hall nearby the Lakeland Rose Show is held each year on the first Friday and Saturday in July.

Haverthwaite village, 'the clearing where oats were grown', is a picturesque cluster of houses and farms south of the main A590 road. Beside one house is a disused lead pump dated 1765. The church, dedicated to St. Anne, stands some little distance from the village and beside the main road. It was built in 1824–5, enlarged in 1827, extended in 1838, and the east end renewed in 1884. A mural tablet tells how a Haverthwaite man, George Dickson, was killed in Montevideo. A shot fired at another man passed right through his body and killed Dickson unintentionally. A slab outside the church is to William Fell, a soldier in the 52nd Light Infantry who fought in many actions during Wellington's campaigns and was several times wounded. Close to the church is the village hall.

The village of Penny Bridge takes its name from the local family

[1] The name fluke comes from the O.E. flóc, a plaice.

of Penny. The banns of marriage of John Penny in 1653 were the first to be proclaimed publicly in the market place of Ulverston as well as in the church. The pub is 'The Britannia Inn'. The church of St. Mary looks down on recent housing development, but has a lovely view northwards towards the Furness Fells. The churchyard is entered through a war memorial lych-gate. The church was first built before 1786 and was consecrated in 1791. It was enlarged in 1831. The present building with its unusual belfry dates from 1856, although the nave was entirely re-built in 1864 at the expense of Countess Blücher von Wahlstadt. There is an ugly 1865 pulpit, with a font to match. The carved oak reredos of 1908 representing the Last Supper is a Machell memorial. The church also serves Greenodd, 'green promontory', and the two villages share a village hall in Greenodd. Greenodd lies along the main A590 road to Ulverston, with one street leading away at an angle. There is a post office, 'The Machell Arms', and 'The Ship Inn'. The village was once quite a busy little port. 'The Ship Inn', built in 1772, was formerly alongside the quay; it has no back door, the rear being built into solid rock.

Newland, on the outskirts of Ulverston, is now only a small cluster of houses on a cul-de-sac from the main road. It had, however, the distinction of possessing the first blast-furnace to be built in the Furness area. The ironworks closed towards the end of the last century. Above the village, on the Hill of Hoad, stands a landmark built in 1850 to resemble Smeaton's Eddystone Lighthouse but never intended as an aid to navigation. It is a memorial to Sir John Barrow (1764–1848), who was born at Dragley Beck about a mile and a half to the south. Barrow was one of the founders of the Royal Geographical Society, and Secretary to the Admiralty from 1804 to 1845. He wrote a book on the mutiny on the *Bounty* published in 1831, as well as several travel books. The climb up to his memorial is rewarded by fine views.

South-east of Ulverston, and just inland from Morecambe Bay, is the quite large residential village of Bardsea, 'Beornred's Island'. Bardsea Hall, for many years the home of the Bardsey family, became a hunting seat and passed into other hands; earlier this century it was demolished. Bardsea Park is now a golf course. There is a post office-store; 'The Ship Inn', and 'The Braddylls

Arms'. The grey stone church with its tall spire and magnificent view over Morecambe Bay was started in 1843 by Colonel Braddyll of Conishead Priory. He failed to finish its construction, and the unfinished church was put up for auction in London. It was bought by the Reverend T. E. Petty who completed it, and became first curate-in-charge. It was consecrated, and dedicated to the Holy Trinity, in 1853. Its lych-gate was erected as a memorial of the church's centenary. The clock in the tower, and a tablet inside the church, commemorate those who died in the 1914–18 war. The sanctuary is an apse. The church has some attractively coloured windows, including some quite modern work. At Sunbrick to the south-west is the Friends' burial ground, where Margaret Fell of Swarthmoor is buried.

Both Baycliff and Scales were hamlets until a short time ago, but have seen considerable residential development during this century. The post office, 'The Farmers Arms', and 'The Fisherman's Arms Hotel' are at Baycliff, which also has a house dated 1659. Scales, 'a hut, or shed', lies inland, spread out on both sides of the road; the school is there.

Tradition has it that all the houses of the old village of Aldingham were swept away in a great tidal wave in 1553. It is very unlikely that the story is true. Aldingham, 'the village of Alda's people', is first mentioned in the Domesday survey of 1086. It is also listed on an inscription in Durham Cathedral as one of the places where St. Cuthbert's disciples rested his body during their flight from the Danes. The church, parts of which are twelfth century, is dedicated to the Saint. There are old stones in the north aisle, including the grave slab of thirteenth-century Goditha de Scales. With them is a more recent statue of St. Cuthbert, with his otters, given to the church by Durham Cathedral. A hole, or hagioscope, permitted worshippers in the south aisle to see the act of the celebration of communion. The chancel arch is crooked—occasionally a feature in old churches, and purporting to symbolize the body of Christ hanging on the cross, head to one side. Queen Victoria, returning from a visit to Furness Abbey in 1848, visited Aldingham church, and the Royal Arms above the chancel arch are hers. The east window, by Harcourt Doyle, is of 1964. In the churchyard is a sundial, and also several seats overlooking the

Bay. Aldingham Hall, almost opposite, was built in the Tudor style for the Reverend John Stonard in 1850. He left it, after his death, to his butler.

Inland again to Gleaston, 'Glasserton' in the Domesday Book. It is a large, straggling, rather nondescript village with a good deal of recent and new residential development. There is a house dated 1686, a post office-store, and 'The Rose and Crown' inn. The village hall is somewhat neglected-looking. The Congregational chapel and school were built in 1887. Half a mile or so north of the village are the remains of Gleaston Castle, now forming part of a farmhouse. It was built by the lords of Aldingham in the fourteenth century, ostensibly as a safeguard against the marauding Scots. It could never have been very strong, however, as its eight- or nine-foot-thick walls were filled only with mud and small stones.

The small farming village of Dendron, 'clearing in the valley', looks quite unimportant. It has, however, close connections with the artist George Romney (1734–1802). Romney was born at Dalton-in-Furness and attended until he was eleven at the village school of Dendron. Between 1642 and 1833 the school was held in the church, built in part for that purpose, as a brass plate formerly above the door but now on the west wall of the nave still testifies; 'This chappell was built and finished in . . . 1642 at the . . . charge of Robert Dickinson, a citizen of London, and borne in the town of Lees . . . to have divine service read . . . according to the Church of England and in the weeke day to have children brought upp in learning and taught therein . . .' The chapel degenerated for a time into a school only, but was re-built in 1767. George Fox preached there in 1652 and says in his *Journal*, 'After this I went to a chapel beyond Gleaston; which was built, but never a priest had preached in it.' The west tower was added in 1833 when the wall which divided the church from the school was removed, and the building was restored in 1891. It is now a small, plain but cared-for church, dedicated to St. Matthew. In the village is a house dated 1726. The present school, and the war memorial, are between Dendron and Leece.

About a mile to the south is the village of Leece where the Robert Dickinson mentioned above was born. The name stands for 'an open place in a wood', and it is twice referred to in Domesday Book as 'Lies'. It is built on a triangle of roads around a pond. There are several eighteenth-century houses, the post office-stores, and 'The Queen's Arms'.

Rampside, 'ram's head', is so called because the promontory on which it stands was thought to resemble the head of a ram. The village is situated at the eastern entrance to Piel Harbour. A tall, square navigational light-tower stands on the sands. Because of its proximity to Barrow much recent residential development has taken place, although there is still one house dated 1654. The pub is 'Clarke's Arms' (presumably named after the family), and the post office is also the village store. The Church of St. Michael stands on its own about three quarters of a mile north of the village and beside the Barrow road. A chapel stood on the same site in 1621, and probably earlier. This was re-built in 1840, and a new chancel added in 1892. In 1909 a Viking sword was discovered in the graveyard. George Fox in his *Journal* records visiting Rampside in 1652. The vicar of the time later joined the Society of Friends.

The pleasant little village of Newton lies between Barrow and Dalton, and not far from Furness Abbey. It possesses a school, dated 1877, a post office-store, and 'The New Commercial Inn'. St. Barnabas church was built in 1899 as a chapel-of-ease to Dalton. Opposite is the village hall and children's playground. The war memorial is enclosed in a small green.

Both names of Stainton with Adgarley, stand more or less for the same thing—'a place on rough, or stony ground', and outcroppings can be seen opposite the two pubs. The village grew up around the quarries and mines. 'The Farmers Arms' and 'The Miners Arms' are virtually side by side in the old village. Newer residential development has taken place away from the old village. Near the pubs is Stainton quarry and also the 1902 Congregational church built to replace the 1873 chapel. The stone for it was given by the Barrow Haematite Iron and Steel Company. A church mission room and school at Adgarley are no longer in use.

The name Urswick stands for 'the village of wild cattle'. Little Urswick is about a mile south-west of Great Urswick, and has its own post office in a private house, and also 'The Swan Hotel'.

It also possesses considerable new housing development. The Recreation Hall is between the two Urswicks. Great Urswick is a larger, rather drab-looking village, spread around three sides of Urswick Tarn. It, too, has a post office. It also possesses 'The Derby Arms' and 'The General Burgoyne Inn', and a small corrugated iron Church of Christ. As at Talkin and Mockerkin a legend of a ruined and sunken village has grown up around its tarn. Presumably, dark shifting shadows, floating weed, and a dread of deep water suggest things to a fanciful mind, but how such stories become firmly based in local folk-lore is difficult to understand. The tale at Urswick is a long and fantastic one. In brief, it tells how the priest in years gone by became convinced of the worthlessness and depravity of the old women of the village, then called Lile Ooston. They demanded a constant supply of water for their cattle, and tested his powers and reviled him. Finally he told them all to go home and open all the windows and doors and stay there for one hour. Turning his back on the village, for he could not bear to see what he knew would follow, the priest induced an earthquake which swallowed all the houses for ever, and when he turned round Lile Ooston had disappeared and in its place was Urswick Tarn. The church does in fact stand at the opposite end of the tarn to the present village. It is a fascinating church, dedicated to St. Mary and St. Michael. A church has been known since pre-Norman times; the present church is ancient, but was restored in 1908. It is entered under a low balcony. The Georgian three-decker pulpit has a 1912 sounding-board in the form of a scallop shell. A hagioscope, or hole in the chancel wall, would enable the occupants of the box pew to see the celebration of mass. There is so much of interest in this church that it is diffito know what to include. Special mention should I think be made of a 1695 brass on the chancel floor which begins with the stern reminder:

> Fond man, why art thou such a sot
> To dote on that which soon is not?
> I mean thy sinful lusts and pleasure,
> Which thou delight'st in above measure.
> Repent in time before too late,
> And think upon approaching fate . . .

Also the unusual and lovely woodcarving, some by the Chipping Camden Guild of Carvers. Particularly good is the large carved figure of a pilgrim, on the left side of the chancel arch, with its accurate costume. The choir stalls have some two dozen smaller carvings of winged children playing musical instruments—the one nearest the organ is of a child with a monkey on an organ. Behind the altar is a painting of the Last Supper by James Cranke (1707–81). Cranke was born, and is buried, at Urswick. He was Romney's early master, and achieved considerable fame in London and in his own district. His artist nephew, also James Cranke (*c.* 1746–1826), is probably better known. He, too, was born at Urswick.

Partly on the A590, and just outside Ulverston, is Swarthmoor, 'black moor'. It has now little appearance of a village, being a concentrated cluster of houses with a great deal of recent development. 'The Red Lion' and 'The Miners Arms' are on the main road. The post office is a private house. The Primitive Methodist Bethel chapel of 1864 is now the Methodist church. The small church of St. Michael and the Holy Angels is a chapel-of-ease to Pennington. It was at Swarthmoor that 2,000 German mercenaries under Martin Swartz camped after landing at Piel in 1487. They had come to help Lambert Simnel in his unsuccessful rebellion against Henry VII. It is, however, for its connection with George Fox and early Quakerism that Swarthmoor is best known. Swarthmoor Hall was the place to which Judge Fell brought his wife Margaret, and the place which George Fox regarded as home even before he married Margaret, then the Judge's widow, in 1669. The Hall is open to the public in the summer months.

Beside the A590 is the war memorial to the men of the village of Pennington. What there is of the spread-out village lies west of the road. The village hall is the Memorial Hall. The pub is 'The Wellington', and there is a post office-store. The church, with stocks outside it, is perched on a hill. It is dedicated to St. Michael and the Holy Angels and was built in 1826 to supersede an older church. Extensive alterations were carried out in 1926. One is instantly struck by the bright colours in the 1971 east window, which is, unusually, a tribute to missionary bishops. A stone tympanum preserved in the church carries an inscription to the effect that 'Gamel founded this church'. It was a Gamel de Pennington, Knight, who founded the hospital which became Conishead Priory.

Also along the A590 is Lindal-in-Furness, 'lime tree valley'. It is a large village at a crossroads. Its rather beautiful village green with trees was at one time a small tarn. The public are kept off it by railings. At one end is the war memorial. Nearby is a house dated 1635, and also the reading room. The Christian Meeting House built in 1875 is now a cleaners. There is a Methodist church of 1871. The village hall is the Buccleuch Hall, and the pubs are 'The Railway' and 'The Anchor Hotel'. The church of St. Peter, built in 1884–6, took the place of an iron building of 1875. It is a cruciform church with the appearance more of a suburban city church than a village church. One gets the impression that the artist of the east window was interested in popularizing moustaches! The only other stained glass is the Holmes Memorial window, an example of work of the 1930s. The school, originally built in 1854 but enlarged several times, is on the Marton road. Marton is a small compact village with little but the pub, 'The New Inn'. Its 1892 Wesleyan chapel is now the Marton Boys' Club.

Ireleth, 'the hill slope of the Irish', is a village on a sharp bend in the A595. It is indeed a 'hill slope', and commands fine views across to Millom, the Duddon Sands, and the Lake hills beyond. The village itself is not attractive. It has a post office-store, and 'The Bay Horse Inn'. There is a barn dated 1762. The 1865 cruciform church of St. Mary serves both Ireleth and Askam, and stands on the edge of Ireleth looking down on both villages. It replaced an Episcopal chapel of 1612 which was used for a time as both chapel and school. It is built of grey limestone and red sandstone and has a memorial tablet to the fallen of the two villages on its south wall. A bell upside down in its churchyard is used as a flower pot, and the old pulpit stands beside it. The rather fine east window is the only stained glass in the church, but I found it a little surprising that the Blessed Virgin Mary is depicted with a *white* rose.

At the bottom of the hill and on the Duddon Sands is Askam-in-Furness. It is a large village, almost a small town, and is virtually joined to Ireleth. It owes its origin to the ironworks, closed since the beginning of the century. In addition to the post office-store there are several other shops; and its pubs are 'The Vulcan', 'The Furness Tavern', and 'The London Tavern'. An ornate drinking fountain was erected for Queen Victoria's Diamond Jubilee in 1897, and the Mission Church carries the same date. There is also a Gospel Hall, a Methodist church 1909, and another one formed from the 1870 Primitive Methodist Zion chapel with a Sunday school added in 1902. A war memorial is in a railed-off green space. I found it an unattractive place, with some quite ugly buildings.

12

From Shap Summit to the Kent Estuary

THIS final chapter covers the long, narrow strip which lies between the M6 motorway and the old A6, the road which for so long was one of the most hated in the country. The delays and frustrations through Kendal, and the winter hazards of Shap Fell, have been replaced by the easy curves and gradients of the most beautifully landscaped motorway in England. All except one of the villages in this section lie to the south of Kendal. That there are not more in the northern half is perhaps hardly surprising when one remembers that it was 1763 before the first stage-coach travelled over Shap Summit.

Exactly halfway (six miles each way) between Kendal and Tebay is Grayrigg, 'grey ridge'. It consists of a few houses, some old, some new, on each side of the A685 road, with views of the hills on both sides. So isolated is the village, that now it has no pub the nearest is in either Tebay or Kendal. The farmhouse at the Lambrigg junction used to be 'The Punch Bowl Inn'. The post office is the last house in the village. The hall is the Coronation Hall, 1911. Opposite is a new primary school, and next to that the rather bleak church dedicated to St. John the Evangelist, built in 1837–8. In 1869 the walls of the tower collapsed and it had to be rebuilt. The church was renovated in 1910. The Society of Friends probably owes its existence to a Grayrigg man, Francis Howgill (1618–69). It was he who introduced George Fox to the 'Seekers' of Westmorland, and they formed the nucleus of the Quaker church. Howgill said of Fox, "God . . . sent one unto us, a Man of God, one of Ten Thousand, to instruct us in the Way of God more perfectly". Howgill was the author of many Quaker writings.

New Hutton is a charming village with a rather ugly village hall. Several of the houses and farms round about date from the sixteenth and seventeenth centuries. It would appear to be a very Royalist village—the small gate leading to the churchyard was erected in 1911 to commemorate the coronation of George V; the church's east window is to 'Queen Victoria the Good'; and the Royal Arms in the church are those of George IV. A lych-gate is in memory of those who fell in the 1914–18 war. The church, dedicated to St. Stephen, was built in 1828–9 to take the place of the 1739 chapel. Apart from the 1906 east window there is no stained glass. There is a rather odd little font in the west end. A board carries the words 'Chapel Wardens Pew 1828'. A double gate outside the church has a greyhound on each gatepost; they face away from each other and one has its tail missing. Similar hounds can be seen on the gateposts of the old village school behind the church. They were the crest of the Sleddall family and came from the old mansion before it was pulled down.

Until the time of Edward I the two Huttons appear to have been one district, and only in about 1297 to have been identified as New and Old Hutton. The present church, replacing several earlier ones, was built in 1873. It is dedicated to St. John the Baptist. Its east end is an apse with just one small window of stained glass. A photograph of a fifteenth-century chalice hangs in the church. It is the oldest piece of church plate in the Diocese, but is no longer in use; it was last used at Easter, in 1874. A simple wooden cross to the fallen of both World Wars is inside the church at the west end. The school next door to the church is of ancient foundation—1613—but has been several times rebuilt and enlarged. Close by is a house carrying a plaque which states that John Wesley lodged there in October 1749, on his way to Leeds from Whitehaven during his first visit to Westmorland. The village hall was built in 1914.

Oxenholme, 'the land where oxen were kept', is an uninteresting place. It is little more than a lot of houses, very many of them recently built, a post office, and a few shops. The pub, 'The

Station Inn', is just outside the village, obviously taking its name from its proximity to the railway station; a main-line station where passengers change for the Windermere line. It was at this station that the Carlisle policeman, P.C. Russell, was shot dead while making an arrest in February 1965. A carved head commemorates him, on the south-east wall of Carlisle Cathedral.

An ancient green surrounded by substantial old stone houses is the focal point of the village of Natland. It is a large village with much new building, including a very modern primary school. The post office is also a general store. The church, of St. Mark, was built in 1909–10 on the site of one built in 1825. Earlier churches had been on a site about one hundred yards away. The theme of deliverance from war seems to permeate the church. The east window is a tribute to all who suffered and endured the 1939–45 war. It is very interesting in its depiction, all along the bottom part, of the various services, civilian and military, all looking upwards with St. George to Christ, while the Holy Spirit hovers above. It was designed by Gerald E. R. Smith. A window in the south aisle is in memory of a father and son—the father was killed in the Battle of the Somme; his boy died of wounds as a prisoner after Arnhem. The two battles are depicted in the glass. One's thoughts go to the woman whose two men were sacrificed so cruelly.

Most of the villages in this part of Cumbria are rather off the beaten track and to some extent isolated. Because of this they are tending to acquire a steady trickle of people from the towns seeking a quieter setting in which to live. Sedgwick, 'the village where sedges grow', is one of these. It is quite a large village with a good deal of new building. It has a post office-general store. There was a gunpowder mill in the village until fairly recently. Sedgwick House, rebuilt in 1869, is now a Lancashire County Council Special School.

A quiet, winding lane leads to the quaint village of Stainton, 'a place on stony ground'. There are new houses, but the village character is quite unspoiled. The Independent chapel built in 1698 is still in use. It was originally 'set apart for religious worship for Protestants dissenting from the Church of England.' Its pulpit is made from part of the original woodwork and bears the date of building. The roof beams also look old. A narrow, seventeenth-century stone footbridge crosses Stainton Beck. There were at one time two mills—a bobbin mill and a corn mill, the latter functioning until as recently as 1951. The school and church are at Crosscrake. The earliest chapel was founded in 1190 and was later looked after by the monks of Furness Abbey. After the suppression of the priory the chapel fell into decay, and remained so until 1757. It was rebuilt in 1773, and then replaced by the present church of St. Thomas in 1875. Of blue Westmorland slate, this gives the appearance of loose stone walling. Inside, it is a light, new, bright church. The only stained glass is in the three windows of the unusually large sanctuary, which also contains stones from the original chapel. The church serves Sedgwick as well as Stainton.

The village of Endmoor lies on the main A65 road from Kendal to Skipton. It is a quite large, and developing, village with several shops, a school, a police station, and a post office. It possesses the Gatebeck Working Men's Club, but its church, and most of the social life of the district, is at Crooklands. 'The Crooklands Hotel' is obviously geared to cater for the busy traffic passing towards the Lakes. Functions take place at the Memorial Hall on the main road. Almost opposite the hall a lane leads up the steep hill to the grey stone church perched at the top, overlooking the motorway and miles of undulating fields. On its tower is a large cross which can be lit up at night to be seen from the motorway. The tower also possesses some gargoyles, from the old chapel dating from the time of Henry VIII which once stood on the same site. There are heads on the sides of all the windows on the south side. Inside, it is a large and pleasant church. Most of its stained glass is of this century, and its carved wooden altar looks modern. A memorial cross in the church bears the names, on brass plates, of the men of the parish who died in both World Wars and there is also a stone memorial cross in the churchyard. The dedication of the church is rather confused. It is the church of Preston Patrick serving several villages and hamlets as well as Endmoor and Crooklands. When it was rebuilt in 1852–3 it appears to have been known as St. Gregory's. The chancel was rebuilt in 1892 and the church apparently renamed St. Patrick's. It was in the old chapel that George Fox preached in 1652 to the 'Seekers' of Westmorland who were to form the nucleus of the Quaker church. Ephraim Chambers, who is referred to under Heversham below, was born at Milton just outside Crooklands.

Hincaster consists of nothing more than a few houses and a telephone kiosk. There is what might have been a village green, with some sort of stone standing in the centre. No one I spoke to had any idea what it was.

Mercifully by-passed by the A6, the small village of Heversham is famous only for its church and its grammar school. Its 'Blue Bell Hotel' is on the A6; the church, a stone's throw away, is not. The post office is opposite the church. The grammar school was founded in 1613 but fell into decay about one hundred years later, to be rebuilt by two old boys—the Bishop of Llandaff and the Bishop of Ferns, in Ireland. The former, Richard Watson (1737–1816), had in fact been born at Heversham. His father was master of the school. He became a professor of chemistry, but his ambition was divinity. He died at Calgarth Park in Westmorland and is buried in Windermere churchyard. A more universally famous pupil was Ephraim Chambers (*c.* 1680–1740) noted for his *Cyclopaedia, or an Universal Dictionary of Arts and Sciences* published in two volumes in 1728 (not to be confused with the better-known *Chambers's Encyclopaedia*). His *Cyclopaedia* went through six editions, was translated into French, and was highly praised by Dr. Johnson. Chambers is buried in the cloisters of Westminster Abbey, and the inscription on his slab was written by himself. The village school, built in 1891, can be seen in a corner of the churchyard. The church is of ancient foundation, and a good deal of its earlier fabric was retained during the major restoration of 1868–71. The old three-decker pulpit was replaced by the present one in 1849. The north chapel oak screen is dated 1605. Near to it is an interesting tablet to Lady Dorothy Bellingham (who died in 1626) with underneath it a small carving of the lady. The reredos is of carved alabaster. There is part of a late ninth-century cross-shaft, which bears some resemblance to Bewcastle Cross. In the churchyard is a 1690 sundial, completely shaded by a huge horse-chestnut tree. The lych-gate was erected in 1894 in memory of a former churchwarden. This is another church with some confusion over its dedication. It is recorded as far back as 1360 as St. Peter's, but some writers have ascribed it to St. Mary.

Milnthorpe, astride the A6 Kendal–Lancaster road, is a busy, grey place, more of a small town than a village by my standards. It has a variety of shops, banks, a police station, a post office, and three pubs—'The Coach and Horses', 'The Bull's Head' and 'The Cross Keys Hotel'. Long queues of cars build up in the summer, and the market square is noisy with cars and people and transistor radios. The eighteenth-century market cross stands west of the square, and is surmounted by a ball, not a cross. The market received its first charter in the thirteenth century. At the opposite side of the square is the church, with the village green in front of it and to one side the war memorial to the 'lads' who gave their lives in the two World Wars. The church was built in 1837 and the interior completely remodelled in 1883. It is dedicated to St. Thomas but this, I understand, was a token not to the saint but to a Mrs Thomasin Richardson who contributed the greater part of its original cost. I have never yet found it open to the casual visitor. Not far away is a new (1969) Roman Catholic church which appears to be of unusual and interesting design. It, too, I have found closed (as is more common with Roman Catholic churches). There is also a Methodist church (1903) and the Kitching Memorial Reading Rooms dated 1880. The name Milnthorpe stands for 'village with a mill'; its wheel presumably driven by the river Bela on which the village stands. It was a place of some importance, even a small port, until the building of the Kendal–Lancaster Canal in 1819 and the construction of the Furness Railway in 1857. A custom which continued until some thirty-five years ago was that 'Shouters' roamed the streets on Christmas and New Year's Eve, calling the names of householders and giving them a traditional greeting. They called the following day for their reward. Constance Holme, the novelist (1879–1955), was born at Milnthorpe.

Still along the busy A6 road is the delightful village of Beetham, a small close-knit village surprisingly quiet for a place so close to a main road. In the summer 'The Wheatsheaf Hotel' caters for a motley collection of travellers. It is set just off the A6. Close by is a very unusual post office, dated 1881 and having above it a block and platform for hoisting up sacks or other goods. Opposite is the ancient and interesting church of St. Michael and All Saints, probably twelfth-century, many times restored. During reconstruction work in 1834 a hoard of about a hundred old coins was discovered at the base of a pillar. These were coins of Edward the Confessor, William the Conqueror and William Rufus. It is a large church. Close to the door is a fourteenth-century vestment chest, and a font with woodwork dated 1636. On display in the south aisle is a Bible of Edward VI (about 1540), believed to be the first English Bible to be used in the church. Between this aisle and the chancel are two much-defaced effigies. There seems to be some doubt whether they are of Sir Thomas Betham and his wife, or of Sir Robert Mydleton and his wife. There is no doubt that the damage was done to them in mid-seventeenth-century by Richard Sill, of Whasset, a feoffee[1] of Beetham School 'who headed a mob and obliged the master and the schollars with some drunken soldiers of Cromwell, or rather Fairfax, to break the painted glass windows and abuse the inside of the church'. It is said that the troops stabled their horses in the church which later had to be re-consecrated. This is why most of the glass is new, with the exception of some fragments near the effigies and containing a portrait reputed to be of Henry IV. Behind the lectern is a wooden cross bearing brass plates, each with the name of a man who died in the two World Wars. The main war memorial stands beside the A6 at its junction with the Arnside road. Dame Clara Butt, the singer, was married in the church in 1900, with Ivor Novello as a page-boy. At the other end of the village beside the A6 are the Church of England Memorial Schools bearing the inscription 'V.R. 1904'—Queen Victoria died in 1901. The name Beetham means 'flat area'.

The country around Beetham is not flat, and the road from there to Arnside is steep and narrow. Arnside itself is a place of steep streets, many of them culs-de-sac, with narrow inter-connecting passages for pedestrians. It is now a large village, almost a small town, and its modern development owes everything to its popularity as a sea-side resort and a place to which people retire,

[1] Feoffee: a person invested with property in land.

despite its hills. It was already a holiday resort in the early part of last century. Its chief remaining link with the past is 'The Fighting Cocks' inn, 1660, still preserved as part of 'The Crown Hotel'. Arnside is the only place where Westmorland touches the sea. The Kent estuary is a birdwatcher's paradise and has been described by Peter Scott as the second most beautiful estuary in the British Isles. It is now spanned by a fifty-arch viaduct, 522 yards long, carrying the Furness Railway over the spot where people either forded, or were ferried over, the Kent. On the hill in the village centre is the large, light, airy church of St. James, built in 1866 and enlarged in 1884, in 1905, and again in 1914. It has a clean polished floor of tiles. What stained glass there is—including on the south side of the altar a window from Holman Hunt's *Light of the World*—is all modern. There is a memorial tablet to the fallen of the two World Wars, with underneath it an open book of remembrance. An excellent idea is the war memorial in the form of playing fields farther into the village. There is also a Methodist church (1875). The Arnside Educational Institute founded almost a century ago is still in use, though with a changed purpose.

Close to the motorway in this southern corner of Westmorland is the village of Holme. It is large, straggling and unattractive, with much typical housing-development of the present century. The older part of the village is slightly more attractive. The pub is 'The Commercial Hotel' with the post office-store nearby. The old National School, established in 1840, appears to be used as the village hall. In front of it stands the war memorial (1923). At the other side of the road is Holy Trinity Church, built in 1839 and restored in 1902. To me it is a stern, harsh church, lacking completely human warmth and kindliness. Even its cleanliness gave the impression that the heart had been scrubbed out of it! I found its three east windows, of 1875, strangely appealing although I do not think they are very good. Behind the pulpit stands a wooden cross about six feet six inches high, bearing a brass plate for each man killed during the 1914–18 war, and a plate for the two men killed between 1939 and 1945. A small wall plaque nearby is surmounted by the British Legion flag. There is also a Methodist church built in 1924.

Index